Music Luminaries praise
MUSIC AND THE 7 HERMETIC PRINCIPLES:

"A fantastic work that bridges the gap between ancient wisdom and modern musicianship."
—Grammy Nominated Composer CLARICE ASSAD

"In an emerging world of AI, this work is an artistic string theory, and a must read for all." —Grammy Finalist Composer/Arranger JOHN LA BARBERA

"I recommend you read this book whether or not you are an artist, because it has something to teach everyone." —saxophonist/composer ALLEN LOWE, author of "Turn Me Loose White Man" Or: Appropriating Culture: How to Listen to American Music, 1900-1960

"Su's book explains how to express your musical story of life on higher levels." —saxophonist ANTOINE RONEY

"Very insightful. It's amazing to me how connected the Hermetic philosophy is to 'modern' science and music." —bassist/composer ASANTE SANTI DEBRIANO

"This is a book I will re-read many times."
—composer/pianist/vocalist LUIZ SIMAS

"This book puts into words the concepts I have always espoused as a musician...it is a cherished and thorough study I'll be referring to for years to come." –composer/pianist PEGGY STERN, founder of Wall St. Jazz Festival and LuluFest.

"Su Terry's 'Music and the 7 Hermetic Principles' is a must-read for musical seekers of today and tomorrow." –pianist BENNY GREEN

"Su Terry has written a fascinating book relating how music is indeed a spiritual journey and one that can be understood in more layman terms, and taught in much detail." –Grammy Award winning trumpeter/composer RANDY BRECKER

"I love this book. It's well-written and touches on very important things." –bassist LONNIE PLAXICO

"Su Terry takes us on an insightful, transcendental journey that examines the wellsprings of creativity and the sonic realities of organized sound. This book offers various strategies that could aid in awakening our collective human intelligence in the face of the current techno age we live in." –pianist JAMES WEIDMAN, Professor of Jazz Piano and African American Studies, University of Georgia

"A *must read* for anyone wishing to explore the deeper relationship between music and the laws of creation." –composer/pianist PAULA KIMPER

"I recommend that musicians take this book to heart." –bassist/producer/educator GENE PERLA

MUSIC
AND THE 7 HERMETIC PRINCIPLES

SU TERRY

MUSIC
and the
7 Hermetic Principles

Ancient teachings for musical minds

Music and the 7 Hermetic Principles: In English. Copyright © 2025 by Su Terry/Qi Note Books, Wilmington, Delaware, USA. All rights reserved. No part of this book may be used or reproduced in any manner whatsoever without written permission except in the case of brief quotations embodied in critical articles and reviews. For information address Qi Note Books, 4023 Kennett Pike, 50013, Wilmington, DE 19807.

First Qi Note Books edition published in 2025. Printed in the United States of America.

Library of Congress Control Number: 2025901302

Print edition ISBN: 978-0-9859245-9-1

Ebook edition ISBN: 978-0-9988844-1-7

Author websites: https://suterry.com
https://templeofartists.substack.com
https://qinote.bandcamp.com

*For my students–
past, present and future.*

CONTENTS

Foreword: xiii

Introduction: xix

Chapter 1: Mentalism 27

Matter and behavior begin with thought. Max Planck said "all matter originates...by virtue of a force which brings the particles of an atom to vibration and holds this most minute solar system of the atom together..." The Hermetic idea "All is Mind" refers to this force: One Mind, the *original* internet cloud. Relationship to Collective Unconscious. Flow states. Integrating isolated sections with the whole piece in a holistic way. Gestalt of music, stage fright, composing from Universal Mind. Is 'mind' the same as 'brain'? "A band is more than the sum of its parts."

Chapter 2: Correspondence 43

The meaning of "as above, so below." Humans are the intermediary between Heaven and Earth. We communicate with the mind of The All and with each form of energy existing on

Earth, including music. The levels of music, improvisation (aka 'spontaneous composition'), playing the unknown, musical signatures, perfect vs relative pitch, moveable vs fixed do. Titles and genres. There are no wrong notes.

Chapter 3: Vibration 59

Tesla said "to understand the Universe, think in terms of energy, frequency and vibration." Nothing is ever at rest. Vibration can both create and destroy. The Law of Attraction. Feeling the vibe, the use of space in music, noticing frequencies in our environment and background music, tuning up, difference tones. Why players of the same instrument sound different. The feeling of silence.

Chapter 4: Polarity 77

There are always two poles to any subject, and all the subject's manifestations are connected by virtue of these poles. The difference is only a matter of degree. Examples of poles by chaos magician Peter J. Carroll. Also, each point on the spectrum has its own polarity. Inversions of musical intervals. Creating passion in performance while maintaining awareness and control. Improvising with the diatonic scale, then adding other intervals. Hindemith–ambiguity of the 3rd. Dynamic range, programming a set, cadences.

Chapter 5: Rhythm 93

"No such thing as absolute rest, or cessation from movement, and all movement partakes of Rhythm." Rhythm doesn't go to the extremes of the poles. Drawing rhythms from nature. People who've lost touch with natural rhythms seek to replace them with excess volume of music. Rhythm in other arts, in spoken language. Being controlled by rhythm. Emotions follow a rhythmic pattern. Recognizing songs by rhythmic pattern alone. Biological rhythms.

Chapter 6: Cause and Effect 107

It seems obvious, but what if it's not? Maurice Nicoll says "in one effect there are many causes." Newton's law. We tend to see time as linear. Linear vs cyclical time. A film and two novels that play with Time. Gurdjieff's Law of Octaves. An ayahuasca experience of Time. Horizontal and vertical aspects of music. Lew Soloff, Philip Glass. No such thing as repetition.

Dimensions in the universe; does music come from another dimension?

Chapter 7: Gender 129

"...any variation of gender can only exist because of its roots in the Masculine and the Feminine. Without this principle there is no Creation." What is mental gender? Far more than a physical reference, the Hermetic idea of gender is understood in terms of correspondences like light/dark, sun/moon, strong/weak, logical/emotional, etc. Interactions of masculine and feminine produce a 3rd force. The anima and animus, other archetypes. The *castrati* in 16th century Italy and their legacy. Chinese philosophy expresses gender in the 'yin-yang' symbol. Blind auditions, equality of male/female personnel in orchestras and venues, female jazz musicians. The role of masculine and feminine in music.

Afterword: 145

Acknowledgements: 147

About the Author: 149

FOREWORD

by Cornelius Boots

As common as music is in people's lives, relatively few people actually spend their entire life devoted to music. Not just committed, not just dedicated, but *devoted* to it. Some of those who do, however, start perceiving deeper layers, holographic dimensions and vast, cosmic implications within what was previously seen as just "music." For example, music is 100% invisible. So it has recently been my position that all musicians are mystics, dealing as we all are with invisible forces. It's basically magic, full stop—no irony or wink needed.

The fabric of this current society, however, has bent the beam of perception in a different direction. It has, in most cases, tricked us into thinking music, like dental cleanings and electronic appliances, is a "good or service." Well, even if it can serve us in that capacity to some extent, the fact remains that deeper layers are unfolding.

Much deeper. Things beyond our narrow focus are playing out.

Enter Su Terry, her lifetime devotion to music, her always-evolving creativity and her spiritual understanding. With *Music & the 7 Hermetic Principles*, she has cleared the path, lit the lights and invited us to slowly but clearly, step-by-step, start seeing the exciting implications of these deeper layers that music both exemplifies and participates in. Deftly mixing insight, clarity and humor, Terry lays out an engaging matrix in this book. The Western occult tradition often runs two conflicting programs simultaneously: enlightening viewpoints, and purposeful obfuscation. Sure, the old *Hermetica* text seems cool, there's certainly some real gold nuggets in there, but who can wade through some of that language? Which translation should you trust? So, we need a guide, someone genuinely interested in amplifying our inner curiosity and intelligence, in contrast to a distant or demi-condescending voice from on-high (which many esoteric thinkers from yesteryear can come across as).

7 Principles is worth taking your own notes as you read, reading it two or three times, and lending it to friends and colleagues. It will present familiar ideas, things you have suspected but never seen spelled out, and perspectives that you would never have come upon anywhere else. In this way, Su has provided a solid bridge that extends both back in time and forward into a new relationship to cosmic, holistic principles. You see, way back in the old days -- both 20,000 years ago and in the 15th century and throughout the Renaissance -- composers and musicians were also doctors, philosophers, sorcerers, scientists and much else besides. Basically, we were ritualistic shamans. Hildegard von Bingen, for example, was a Christian, a profound composer and an influential mystic.

Later on, Renaissance magicians like Agrippa and Ficino were active composers while also publishing some of the seminal texts on occult philosophy that directly shaped Western magical thought, which in turn laid the foundation for what we today call "science." Alchemy itself was a kind of global interest as it was a prominent practice among philosophers and magicians in both the West and the East. And by the way, most music outside of the so-called Western world was never separated from its magical and sacred role. Similarly Zen, Taoism and many Eastern philosophies in general have remained much more holistic, grounded and interested in balance and vitality. And, in spite of the secular pallor ascribed to most music these days, much of Western (i.e. European) music is sacred at its root: the polyphony of Notre Dame, the Mass itself, or the Greeks, who were famously leading mytho-scientifical lives.

The twist came when our analytical left-brain took over completely, rewrote history and took a scalpel to all that groovy, magical, allegedly "woo woo" stuff. If you can't kill it, dice it and measure it, it ain't "real," this sociopathic influencer tries to tell us. Don't believe that socio-mental propaganda! Paracelsus and Newton, fathers of "modern" science were, in fact, alchemists and Rosicrucians. They were into some very out there spiritual and magical viewpoints and practices. Emanuel Swedenborg in the 18th century flowed back the other direction: he was a top mineralogy scientist for the Swedish government when he started having mystical visions and ongoing conversations with angels, which he continued to document and categorize in the same meticulous and thorough manner with which he had approached the natural sciences. Moving into the 20th century and returning directly to musicians, both Su and I have been profoundly influenced and inspired by creative woodwinders such as Rahsaan Roland Kirk, Eric Dolphy, John Coltrane and many others who centralized nature, cosmic consciousness, dreams, spirituality and mysticism within both their lives and their music.

The point is: that which has been fragmented and torn asunder must be put back together again for us to ascend up the spiral. We have 7 tones in many of our scales, 7 days of the week, 7 colors in the rainbow; perhaps we need 7 principles around which to organize our exploration of the deeper layers of music. 7 access points to the Great Mystery. Stay curious! I hope you find your mind and your heart resonating with these 7 principles as Su Terry illuminates the way.

"Just let your mind wander along in the drift of things. Trust yourself to what is beyond you – let it be the nurturing center."
  - Zhuangzi: the Inner Chapters [trans. D. Hinton]

Cornelius Boots
Founder, Black Earth Shakuhachi School
Friday the 13th of September, 2024
Jenkintown, Pennsylvania

AUTHOR'S INTRODUCTION

As both a musician/composer and a spiritual seeker, I've spent my life investigating the connections between music, metaphysics and spirituality. If we see spiritual life as being the larger whole, then certainly music is a microcosmic expression of that whole.

The relationships that play out in music—between notes, between harmonic structures, between rhythm figures—seem to echo relationships between people and things: there is attraction and repulsion, consonance and dissonance, tension and release.

No less are dynamics represented, from pianississimo to triple forte and everything in between. Texture, phrasing, repetition, pattern recognition, tone color, voicing. . . every possible musical element is but a representation of the larger world around us.

Today's musicians face immense challenges in terms of finding performance venues, marketing our music, and navigating the digital world, including AI offerings increasingly used to replace human musicians. We also have the traditional challenge of always seeking to improve our musicianship and our musical abilities.

This book addresses the latter. But because of the former, many of us feel even more driven to find and express what is uniquely human in music–the depth of emotion, understanding and wisdom that cannot, nor will ever be, expressed or replicated by a robot or computer program.

This is not to say that we don't welcome and use the tools offered by computer programs in the creation of our works, whether in composition, live performance, or recordings. Of course we do! We are creative beings and we use any useful tools that are available to us.

What we wish to avoid is turning over the reins of the creative process to these programs. There is no reason to do that. Instead, let's apply the wisdom of the ages so we can

Introduction

continue to develop our extraordinary human potential. Sages of both recent days and remote antiquity knew how to access the source of such wisdom. It is to them we turn for guidance. Hence this work on the 7 Hermetic Principles and how they relate to music.

The Hermetic literature has its origin in a mysterious figure named Hermes Trismegistus, meaning "Hermes Thrice-Great." This Hermes has come down to us through history as something of a composite character, merging the Egyptian god Thoth with the Greek god Hermes. Regardless of his quasi - fictional nature, Hermes Trismegistus became the figurehead named as author in much of the Hermetic literature. This is in keeping with the spiritual tradition of students and scholars preferring to remain anonymous, instead naming a revered authority as the writer.

The Hermetic texts originated in ancient Alexandria in Egypt, proceeding through the ages to places like 12th century Arabia and the Italian Renaissance, eventually landing in the 19th century New Thought movement in the United States. These texts are considered important to both the Western theological and alchemical traditions–and what is music if not an alchemical process that transforms 'sound elements' through various combinations, thereby transforming not only the performer but the listener as well?

The texts I have consulted for this work include the Greek *Corpus Hermeticum* and Latin *Asclepius* (Brian P. Copenhaver translation), the *Nag Hammadi Library*, *The Secret History of Hermes Trismegistus* by Florian Ebeling, *The Hermetica: The Lost Wisdom of the Pharaohs* by Timothy Freke and Peter Gandy, the *Kybalion,* and a dozen translations of the *Emerald Tablet* from different eras in history.

As with the Bible, these texts of different eras have branched out in various directions, yet they share the concept of acquiring wisdom through revelation, secrecy, and initiation. In fact, the spiritual and philosophical value of these texts doesn't even stem from their alleged authorship by the legendary Hermes Trismegistus, but rather in the verifiable truths they contain.

Introduction

What I have selected as the main focal point for the present book is the compilation of Hermetic Principles stemming from the New Thought movement and published as *The Kybalion.* Some ardent Hermetic scholars may regard this collection as the 'least authentic' of the available Hermetic texts. Nevertheless, as a compendium of Hermetic ideas, its influence on modern spiritual and metaphysical thought is undeniable. Moreover, its straightforward presentation of spiritual principles is so relatable to musical principles that studying them cannot fail to inform and inspire us.

From the verse "Secret Teachings" of the *Hermiticum*:

Atum's (God's) grace never fails
and there is no end to his bounty.
He is by nature a musician
who composes the harmony of the Cosmos
and transmits to each individual

Music and the 7 Hermetic Principles

the rhythm of their own music.
If the music becomes discordant,
don't blame the musician,
but the lyre-string he plays,
that has become loose and sounds flat,
marring the perfect beauty of the melody.

But I have noticed
that when an artist deals with a noble theme
his lyre becomes mysteriously tuned,
so that its deficiencies
issue glorious music,
to the amazement of his listeners.
It has been like this with me.
I confess my weaknesses,
but by Atum's power
my music is made good,
and he will likewise
make your music perfect.

–translation by Timothy Freke and Peter Gandy
- *The Hermetica: The Lost Wisdom of the Pharaohs.*

Introduction

"Knowing music is nothing more than being versed in the correct sequence of all things together as allotted by divine reason. By divine song, this sequencing or marshalling of each particular thing into a single whole through reason's craftwork produces a certain concord - very sweet and very true."

– translation of the Asclepius chapter from the Brian P. Copenhaver *Hermetica*, published by Cambridge University Press.

HERMETIC PRINCIPLE 1:

MENTALISM

"The All is Mind; the Universe is Mental." –The Kybalion

All matter and all human behavior begin with thought. We've heard this idea before. It is espoused not only by New Age pundits, but also in Biblical verses and other ancient texts.

Max Planck, a revered physicist of the early 20th century, said the following in his book *The New Science*:

"As a man who has devoted his whole life to the most clearheaded science, to the study of matter, I can tell you as a result of my research about the atoms this much: There is no matter

as such! All matter originates and exists only by virtue of a force which brings the particles of an atom to vibration and holds this most minute solar system of the atom together. . . . We must assume behind this force the existence of a conscious and intelligent Mind. This Mind is the matrix of all matter."

Planck's statement echoes the ancient Hermetic principle of Mentalism. Notice that he refers to what Hermetic adherents call 'One Mind.' We interpret the phrase 'all is mind' not according to an individual's small mind, but rather the mind belonging to "The All." The All refers to the Force uniting everything in the Universe. Some have called this force "God" or "Spirit" or "The Tao." As with the Hermetic term 'Mind,' The All is not a personal force. Neither is it anything that can be prayed to. (This is not to suggest that prayer doesn't work, as we'll explore further in the Principle of Correspondence chapter.) Rather, it is an impersonal force within which all the energies of the Universe circulate. The term 'Mind' is used as a descriptor because The All contains everything and is ultimately unknowable—just as the mind of a human being has seemingly infinite layers, some of which are quite hidden and only show themselves under certain conditions, if ever.

Another aspect of the Hermetic principle of Mentalism is that each manifestation we see in our own plane of existence is a small bit of The All. A tree, a person, a worm, a table, a saxophone, a vapor, a sound, a memory, a thought—all of these are part of The All.

Some might liken the Mind of The All to Carl Jung's concept of the Collective Unconscious, which is a repository of images and archetypes shared by the entirety of humanity. As such, one's individual mind is connected not only to all other individual minds, but also to the collective mind. In a way the Internet 'cloud' where we store data is mimicking the ability of humans to connect with each other, and with the Mind of The All. So the 'cloud' didn't originate with computers—humans had it first!

Another way of putting it is that anything existing on the physical plane, first exists on the mental plane. For example, we imagine our compositions in our mind before writing them down. We hear them internally. We don't necessarily need the reference of an instrument (e.g. a piano) to hear the relationships, we have already 'internalized' them.

Think of Beethoven; everything he composed during the last four years of his life, including Symphony No. 9, was composed when he was completely deaf!

When we speak of Mentalism in music, the first and most obvious application is that to play music, we have to think in the language of music. Superimposing another language on it, like mathematics or English, will not do at all. Music is its own language and we must be thinking in music when we're playing music. This concept could be extended to say we must be thinking in music when we're listening to music, even if we're not playing.

"Mastery is playing whatever you're capable of playing—every time—without thinking."
-Kenny Werner

Mentalism

Every good musician has had the experience of "being one" with the music they're playing, even if it is rare. In those moments we feel as if we're inside the music, and the music is inside us. There is no differentiation. When one is fluent in a language, one just flows with it in conversation and doesn't need to mentally translate any parts of it to a different language.

Athletes experience this state as well, and they call it "being in the zone." Because this state is a state of inclusiveness rather than separation, there are paradoxes. Former pro tennis player and musician Torben Ulrich, who during his career was a guru for a number of young tennis players, puts it this way:

When hitting the ball
has become nothing special
that's the time
to stop.

When hitting the ball
has become nothing special
that's the time
to really hit it.

If we were to adapt this poem to the subject of music, we might say:

When playing
has become nothing special
that's the time
to stop.

When playing
has become nothing special
that's the time
to really play.

Musicians live for those moments of being in the zone. For most of us they don't happen often enough, and we can easily play a whole gig or concert without ever reaching that state. Thankfully, the state is completely subjective to the player. The audience has no idea whether or not the musician is in the state, and excellent music can even be played at a high level without any of the players being in that state. That said, when one or more players is indeed in the zone, it communicates not only to the other players but to the audience as well. And one player reaching the state makes it easier for others in the ensemble to reach it also.

Another term for this altered state of consciousness, where one feels union with the thing one is doing, is "Flow" or "Flow State." This term has been popularized by the microdosing and biohacking communities who have developed a number of protocols designed to facilitate entering the Flow.

All experienced musicians have had moments when they felt they were not playing the music, but rather the music was playing them. This is being connected to Mind in its larger sense. While in this flow state, playing music is effortless. The paradox is that this effortless feeling has been achieved through much effort!

Another way we can apply the principle of Mentalism to music is in our training process (practicing). We use it when we're confronting a challenging passage or exercise in order to assimilate the phrase into our overview or skillset. Even less advanced players can learn how to do this. When we come across a difficult passage, it needs to be dissected to establish where is the weak link in the chain. Usually it's a skip between two notes, an awkward fingering, or a lack of proper articulation (oftentimes just articulating the right notes in a passage makes it way easier to play).

Once the passage has been analyzed in this way and the problem spots corrected, we integrate the phrase back into the whole piece. When we do this we think in "music." That passage we have worked so hard on cannot ever be thought of as separate from the rest of the piece (although we could also make it into an exercise and transpose it into all keys!)

So how do we re-integrate the isolated phrase with the entire piece? When we focus on details in music, it's easy to get lost in those details. It's possible to go into a sort of obsessive compulsive behavior pattern just working on a fingering or an articulation over and over and over. But because All is Mind, we don't want to do things mindlessly, including practicing. We have to zoom in and zoom out at the same time. We zoom in to focus on correcting or enhancing a passage, but we also have to have the big picture of how that passage fits in with the entire piece. When we analyze a specific passage we're working on, we simultaneously hold onto the entire piece in our mind, so that the passage doesn't become its own thing. Everything is connected, always.

Perhaps a more readily understood term would be that we're using a holistic approach to learning the piece. The ubiquitous term 'holistic' refers to the principle All is Mind. We're even starting to see a return to holistic approaches in Western medicine even though it's still the minority. Somehow the ancient knowledge that 'everything is connected' has gotten a bit lost in the current era of specialization!

The 1920s spiritual Dem Bones, a traditional theme collected by James Weldon Johnson and J. Rosamond Johnson, expresses this view:

Toe bone connected to the foot bone
Foot bone connected to the heel bone
Heel bone connected to the ankle bone
Ankle bone connected to the leg bone

Leg bone connected to the knee bone
Knee bone connected to the thigh bone
Thigh bone connected to the hip bone
Hip bone connected to the back bone
Back bone connected to the shoulder bone
Shoulder bone connected to the neck bone
Neck bone connected to the head bone
Hear the word of the Lord.

Max Wertheimer (1880-1943) was one of the founders of Gestalt psychology. He studied music as a young man. He said "what is given me by the melody does not arise ... as a secondary process from the sum of the pieces [sections] as such. Instead, what takes place in each single part already depends upon what the whole is."

This idea is sometimes summarized as "the whole is more than the sum of its parts." Or as I like to say, "a band is more than the sum of its parts." I have been in many bands, and have seen firsthand how the right combination of members creates a chemistry that elevates the band as a whole entity. It confers a power to the band that emanates not from the individual members on their own, but only through their musical interaction with each other.

Since Universal Mind conveys the feeling of being connected to everything, including the audience, it's not possible to feel performance anxiety (aka 'stage fright') when you're in that state. Feeling anxious when performing comes from a sense that you are separate from the audience, separate from The All, as well as separate from the music itself. (You are playing the music instead of the music playing you.)

In contrast, when you feel connected to the audience and the music, and you are just part of a giant wheel with spokes emanating from your center out to everything else, anxiety doesn't even enter the picture. You could also imagine, instead of spokes radiating from your center, that they are radiating from Universal Mind and you are inside that. Both are true. Use whatever works for you.

"The finest of matter is air, the finest air is soul, the finest soul is mind and the finest mind is god."

—*Hermetica.* Discourse of Hermes Trismegistus: On the mind shared in common, to Tat

Let's address a question that may be lurking behind the scenes: Is 'mind' the same as 'brain'?

No. 'Mind' is a much larger concept—huge, gargantuan, humongous! The way sages and seers refer to 'Mind' is in the sense of the power that created the Universe. In terms of a human being, 'mind' can be said to be the entire physical, mental and emotional system of that being. (Therefore when we learn to cultivate awareness of this system and connect its parts, we can achieve seemingly miraculous abilities.) The ability to play music comes from this Mind. At the same time, the individual mind is connected to other individual minds. And beyond that, individual minds are connected to The All. Which is the ultimate Mind.

The All is said to be unknowable because we can't separate ourselves from it in order to analyze it. To quote Max Planck again, from his book *Where Is Science Going*:

Mentalism

Science cannot solve the ultimate mystery of nature. And that is because, in the last analysis, we ourselves are a part of the mystery that we are trying to solve.

This statement goes along with the Heisenberg Principle, an important component of Quantum Physics which says that of the two descriptors of a particle (position in space, and velocity) we can only fully know one of them at a time. The more we know about the position of the particle, the less we know about its velocity– and vice verse. The very process of observing the particle involves us in that process, so that "we ourselves are a part of the mystery that we are trying to solve."

Just as the Universe is a mental projection in the mind of The All, so also is music a projection coming from the mind of the composer. Even if the piece is improvised, it's still being composed, albeit spontaneously. So music is very much a projection that comes from Mind.

Composers often do not know where some of their compositional ideas came from!

That's a result of being open to receive ideas from the Mind of The All. (But this defense might not work in a copyright infringement trial, which is why we have music licensing services when we want to record music written by someone else. ("Your Honor, I swear I didn't know my hit song was already recorded by Stevie Wonder in 1961. I got it from Universal Mind!")

All is Mind. The Universe is Mental. Music is Mind. The Universe is Music.

Reader comments

Marco Romano: The second Max Planck quote reminded me of this Jung quote: "There is no Archimedean point from which to judge, since the psyche is indistinguishable from its manifestations. The psyche is the object of psychology, and-fatally enough-also its subject. There is no getting away from this fact."

George Neidorf: The first time I entered into that flow was in the 7th grade. In the band room, after school. a saxophone player (Joe Mericle. Now there's a name) started playing in the manner of Big Jay McNeely, Joe Houston, et al. We played as fast as we could, and at one point I felt like I was being played and watching myself playing. I had to wait for another 10 years for that to happen again. After that, whenever I played with Cedar Walton it happened. These, playing by myself, and focusing on the sounds I'm making, I can easily enter that state. When bits of me start to reappear I know it's time to stop. Thinking is the curse of the improviser.

Connie Cheng: Zooming in and out in practice is hard to do. At this point in journey I've had small moments of flow, like when another musician took the music in a different direction and somehow something interesting and "new" came out of me... but not yet at the point where I can let go all the time or trust that! Indeed much to know before I can play as if not knowing.

Music and the 7 Hermetic Principles

HERMETIC PRINCIPLE 2:
CORRESPONDENCE

"To obtain a correct idea of the construction of the Microcosm, we should know how the Macrocosm is constructed; we must look upon man as an integral part of universal Nature, and not as something separate or different from the latter."
–Paracelsus, *Paragran*.

The Principle of Correspondence entered popular speech in the axiom "As above, so below." It works both ways, so the complete phrase is "As above, so below. As below, so above."

Astrology works along the Principle of Correspondence. Popular media, too, often portrays the Principle of Correspondence in action, as in science fiction movies where the beings on other planets behave exactly the same as people on Earth. They exhibit all our emotions: jealousy, anger, hatred, love, tenderness, joy and sadness. They are just as territorial and possessive, nationalistic, racist, secretive and warlike as we are. And if the famous Star Wars bar scene is any indication, apparently they like to drink.

There really is no difference in saying "as above so below" or "as below so above." These are just reflections of each other. When the ancient Greeks and Romans created myths of gods and their interactions with humans, they ascribed to the gods the same attributes they saw in their fellows. Equally so in other cultures, where the activities of the higher spirits form a direct correlation with the humans below, and offer an explanation of natural phenomena based on the same characteristics that humans are familiar with from their own species.

Correspondence

The great Second Hermetic Principle embodies the truth that there is a harmony, agreement, and correspondence between the several planes of Manifestation, Life and Being. This truth is a truth because all that is included in the Universe emanates from the same source, and the same laws, principles, and characteristics apply to each unit, or combination of units of activity, as each manifests its own phenomena upon its own plane.
—*The Kybalion*

By referring to correspondences we are not separating anything from anything else. To the contrary: we are establishing relationships between Above and Below (and by extension, Within and Without). What connects the two realms? We do. Humans are the intermediary between Heaven and Earth. While the previous chapter on Mentalism states that The All is not something that we can pray to for specific outcomes, nevertheless there is a correspondence between energies that exist on

Earth, and cosmic energies. Author Gregg Braden describes prayer as a feeling rather than a set of words (although the feeling may be accompanied by words if we wish). Because of the Plane of Correspondence, the energetic feeling of a prayer may be communicated to The All. The Principle of Vibration, discussed in a later chapter, can then replicate that energetic feeling on all levels so that we feel our prayer has been answered.

It's not very mysterious at all. Just about everything we experience on earth, as humans, is a type of energy. Heat, electromagnetism and gravity are familiar to us as forms of energy, but equally so are emotions and thoughts. Even the realm of physical objects sees those objects as forms of energy, since they are made up of vibrating particles we call by names like electrons, neutrons, and so forth. These are just names for energies, because humans love to name and classify everything; the energy itself doesn't need a name.

There are many factors that influence the movement of energy. We know from personal experience that music is one of these factors.

Correspondence

How would we apply the Principle of Correspondence to music? When we're playing or listening to music, there are elements we understand and can follow easily, and there are other elements we aren't familiar with or that we can't explain. Some listeners enjoy only the most consonant harmonies and lyrical melodies, and if the music goes beyond Mozart, Haydn or Vivaldi they're lost. They would never voluntarily listen to Stockhausen or Boulez. Although such a listener might appreciate more modern music if it doesn't stretch their boundaries too much. Debussy or Arvo Pärt might be more accessible to them because the complexity of that music is, in a sense, hidden behind a softer presentation.

Yet if lovers of Wolfgang Amadeus M. invested the energy in understanding how Karlheinz S. uses the exact same musical principles–just expressed differently–they might appreciate the latter a bit more!

In jazz this can be seen by contrasting Dixieland and Swing Era music with the bebop period that followed. Indeed, the traditional musicians themselves objected to bebop when it first came out. It challenged their understanding of melody, harmony, rhythm, texture, tension and release, and all the other musical elements that were instinctive to them in their own genre but now seemed unrecognizable.

There are also levels of correspondence. We can't just point to one thing that's 'above' and another that is 'below,' because where does the earth end and the sky begin? Inside what we call 'above' are levels. Likewise in the 'below' realm. Music is a microcosmic expression of the macrocosm, but it's also its own macrocosm. Musically speaking we might refer to the overall structure and melody of a song as 'above' and the individual elements contained therein as 'below.' Or the opposite! A good piece of music will have individual elements that reflect the structure and melody. Likewise, contemplation of the structure and melody enables us to express the individual elements properly.

Even the title of the piece can provide an access point to understanding it. Suppose a listener feels a piece in the style of *Musique Concrète* is 'above' them. Or an opera fan feels

Correspondence

a heavy metal selection is 'below' them. The title of the song may not get listeners to like it, but it can give them a clue as to what the piece is about.

A piece with a lot of dynamic movement, fast tempo, or quick passages with 16th notes or 32nd notes, bold textural statements and sudden dynamic changes might be described by different listeners as aggressive, adventurous, angry, exploratory, overwhelming, cinematic, or any number of similar adjectives. Such a piece of music might generate titles like *Up Against the Wall, Fighting the Dragon, Mount Everest or Bust, New York IRT line*, etc. Since music is the ultimate expression of the unification of Above and Below, it gives us what we need–whether we want it or not.

We need differences in order to have understanding. Through differences we learn who we truly are. The Principle of Correspondence helps us understand the relationship between apparent differences and how they can be unified, just as the inversions of intervals, melodies and chords only exist because of their non-inverted states.

There's another correspondence we must mention, and that is the relation of the known to the unknown. This relationship becomes especially important in improvised music, because the players who are spontaneously composing ("spontaneous composition" is a more accurate term than "improvisation") must play what is unknown. That is, they must play things that have not been previously delineated. In order to do this, a good improvisor calls on their knowledge of compositional elements and techniques to express musical ideas that essentially come from the cosmos, but have been refined by humans over the centuries.

Should the word "cosmos" offendeth thee, we could say these musical ideas come from the Collective Unconscious of humanity, a realm rich with all manner of imagery and sound according to Carl Jung, who coined the term in the first place.

Musical ideas expressed in spontaneous composition/improvisation are unknown to the player in advance, unlike "known" elements such as notes and rhythms previously written down or otherwise codified. But because the principle of Correspondence exists, we're able to extract elements of the unknown and make them knowable. What could be cooler than that?

Conversely, it's possible that known elements can disappear from that realm and retract into the unknown. This has happened countless times, as when a past civilization disappears and there is not even a record of it having ever existed. Then Graham Hancock goes to a place like Göbekli Tepe on an expedition, writes about the civilization in a book, does a TV show about it, and all of a sudden it's common knowledge again!

Dating back to Ancient Egypt, the Hermetic Principles are also associated with alchemy, the science of transformation. Alchemy as an art and science reached its pinnacle in the Middle Ages and the Renaissance, and one of its legends is the great Swiss physician Paracelsus (c. 1493-1541). His alchemical and hermetic training gave him an insight into the correspondence between the characteristics of a plant and symptoms of illness in a human being. He coined the term "signature" for any characteristic of a substance, such as the habitat in which a plant grows and in what season, or its form, or the color of its flowers. The concept of signatures is today widely used in homeopathy.

In music we also have signatures. The most obvious example can be found in musical octaves, where the same note sounds at a number of different levels, both lower and higher in pitch. Human societies may divide their octave into differing intervalic relationships, but they all recognize the repetition of the octaves and place their scales inside that framework. We recognize a note as "repeating" in its octaves because it has a signature corresponding to its frequency relationships. The signature is echoed in each octave.

Each pitch has its own signature. In our Western system of 12 notes per octave, the sequence of these pitches is called the Chromatic Scale. The name "chromatic" refers to color. Each note has its own sound color, hence the 'chromatic scale.' Persons who are able to name any note they hear without reference to an instrument are said to have 'perfect pitch,' meaning that they hear the 'color' of the note. When we're kids we learn to associate the frequencies of colors with names like 'red,' 'blue,' or 'yellow' and we can do the same with pitch colors. Certain languages—Chinese for example—even use pitched inflections which indicate the meaning of words. With pitched inflections being part of the language, it's no surprise to find so many Chinese musicians in the classical music world. Since children growing up in China are exposed to subtle variations in pitch (in the form of language) immediately upon birth—or even in the womb—they are more disposed to developing perfect pitch.

Perfect pitch is not only an innate talent; a degree of it can indeed be cultivated. (It's not easy though.) Research shows about 1 in 10,000 people have perfect pitch, although the ability is really not that useful. Musicians benefit far more from cultivating good relative pitch, having to do with the relationships of pitch intervals. A strong foundation in relative pitch solidifies itself in the Principle of

Correspondence and serves for a musician's entire life.

In the world of jazz, we have an interesting phenomenon that can be attributed directly to the Principle of Correspondence. During an improvisational (or 'spontaneously composed') section, it may happen that a 'wrong note' is played. Although I've said many times there are no wrong notes, only notes we didn't intend to play, we still may wish to 'correct' that note. But how do we do that when the note has already been played? The clam has already opened its shell–there's no going back! Or is there?

This actually happens all the time, and here's how we deal with it: after we play the note that we didn't intend to play, we play something else after it that makes it sound as if we did intend to play it! It's similar to making a faux pas in conversation, then saying something else that mitigates your error. Obviously the art of transforming a mistake into an expression of genius–or at least lessening its cringe factor– takes a great deal of skill and experience. But yes, it can be done and in fact is done quite often.

In the context of a musical improvisation, all the levels of music must be taken into account. An improvisor who only operates on one level is a poor musician. We operate on all the levels simultaneously because that's part of the language of music. This is what enables a good improvisor to correct a wrong note after it's been played, among many other skills. The musical 'big picture' includes all the levels, so we can bring an element from one level into another level, thus unifying the bad note into a context where, in retrospect, it was a good note. Maybe even a better note!

We could also say that the moveable-*do* system of sight singing, as opposed to the fixed-*do* system, is a tool of the Principle of Correspondence. With moveable-*do*, all the relationships between intervals stay the same no matter what key we're in, because we indicate the root with "*do*." We may have to use fixed-*do* (always using "C" as "*do*") when dealing with certain contemporary or avant-garde pieces though, as those genres tend to emphasize other musical principles like texture and dynamics over lyricism and melodic repetition. (We can relate such a situation to the times when Newtonian physics is a more useful descriptor of physical reality than Quantum physics.)

Again, the best use of the Principle of Correspondence is having a 'big-picture' of how different levels can inform each other. As we strive to make sense of an increasingly chaotic world with its proportional increase in sense impressions, the Principle of Correspondence shows us a great Truth: As above, so below; as below, so above.

Reader comments

Mary-Lou: What the arts do is to give us the opportunity to go beyond one's self, both for the artist and for the audience: a shared transcendental experience, where your expression resonates in my soul. and very true also: it is about the harmonies we perceive, a.k.a. the vibrations of the universe, a.k.a. the waves (measurable in a sinus/co-sinus graph) of sound, movement, colour, form, texture - including the 'disharmonies' (which is a subjective category, as you also mentioned). central to all is, perhaps, that

Correspondence

wondrous idea we call the Divine Inspiration, a pathway to open one's self to the forces beyond our direct, earth-bound existence. we might call it Nature, God, or the 9 Muses (Clio, Thalia, Erato, Euterpe, Polyhymnia, Calliope, Terpsichore, Urania, Melpomene), what you will. and that one "wrong" note you thought you heard? intentional, my dear Watson!

George Neidorf: One afternoon, while listening to a Stockhausen piece, with the window open, all the sounds that I could hear from outside, fit perfectly with the music. The Stockhausen piece Zyklus, for solo percussionist, is spiral bound and you may start on any page and continue until you come back to the beginning. The composer said, "You can turn the pages clockwise, towards ever increasing certainty, or counterclockwise, towards ever increasing ambiguity."

Music and the 7 Hermetic Principles

HERMETIC PRINCIPLE 3:
VIBRATION

"If you wish to understand the universe, think in terms of energy, frequency and vibration".
– Nikola Tesla

With the third Hermetic principle we come to a concept that is already well known in the world of music: vibration. (Another musical term, "rhythm," will be discussed with the fifth principle.)

The Principle of Vibration says that nothing is ever at rest. Solid matter is an illusion that we maintain on the macrocosmic level. At the microcosmic level, all matter is composed of oscillating atoms and molecules, which are just terms for energy groupings.

From corpuscle and electron, atom and molecule, to worlds and universes, everything is in vibratory motion. This is also true on the planes of energy and force (which are but varying degrees of vibration); and also on the mental planes (whose states depend upon vibrations); and even on to the spiritual planes...he who understands the Principle of Vibration has grasped the sceptre of power...
–The Kybalion

Vibration can both create and destroy. Vibration changes something from one state into another state. Soldiers in the infantry know they must break step when crossing a bridge, otherwise the vibration created by multiple synchronized footfalls may collapse it.

The Law of Attraction, much bandied-about in modern times, is part of the Principle of Vibration. In order to achieve something or acquire something you must match its vibration. You cannot be One with something unless you

Vibration

are sharing its frequency. Because we have a certain vibration, we attract whatever matches that vibration. That puts us in sync with it–or in harmony with it, to use another musical term.

We can speak of vibrations in a physical way, but they also manifest on the emotional and spiritual planes. In the 1960s and 70s it was popular to speak of someone's personal "vibe." This can be extended to refer to the feeling in a certain place, such as a restaurant. Today we're more likely to use an expression like "I really resonate with that" to describe how we feel about a given subject. The word 'resonance' describes a relationship between two things whereby they're in sympathetic vibration. Technically, what's happening is that an existing oscillation is amplified by an external oscillation that matches its natural frequency, or a harmonic of it.

A note sung or played in a room with a violin, piano, guitar or drum will create a sympathetic vibration in those instruments when it's the same as the note the string or drum head is tuned to. Vibrations must match, or there will be no resonance. (Although there can also be resonance with the initial harmonics of the overtone series, since the overtones are present in each fundamental tone. To test this, strike a low key on a piano and hold it. You should be able to discern a minimum of two or three harmonics sounding right along with it.)

In relation to the Law of Attraction we hear phrases like "tuning in" which come from the technologies of radio and television. There are many channels, all broadcasting at the same time. In order to view or listen to the channel we want, we must tune in to its specific frequency. If we don't like what's playing, we change the channel.

This concept also applies to our life in general. We can't manifest more money unless we're vibrating at the "money" frequency. We stop vibrating at the "lack" frequency and start vibrating at the "abundance" frequency.

Remember the first Hermetic principle, All is Mental. Our thoughts (and actions based on those thoughts) create specific vibrations that attract similar vibrations, whether 'good' or 'bad.' Universal laws are impartial; they don't

Vibration

judge whether something is good or bad—only humans do that.

Yet the Law of Attraction doesn't seem to work for some people. Even after they've watched The Secret ten times, and read all of the Abraham-Hicks books! Why is that? After all, shouldn't a Universal Law always work? Yes and no. As with any principle, it must be understood in its entirety in order to apply it to one's life. I believe the mistake people make is not realizing that one must apply the Principle of Vibration to what is there, but also to what is not there—and the two must be balanced. Just as music has notes and rests, the Law of Attraction has the thing that is desired, and the space that exists to accommodate the thing when it shows up.

We're very familiar with the things we desire. We contemplate them, research them, dream about them, hope for them. But we often do nothing about nurturing the space which has to hold those things. The space cannot be considered as empty, as lacking the thing we want. Rather, it has to also contain the vibration of the thing. The space attracts, because the space is what will be filled with the thing we desire.

If nothing else, the space is where we can take actions toward the goal we're seeking. We make space for this in our days, every day.

In music, space is rests. Space is breath. Space is phrasing. Space primes the listener for the action that is to come as the music unfolds in time. The element of space in music is a big part of what makes it musical.

Thirty spokes share the wheel's hub;
It is the center hole that makes it useful.
Shape clay into a vessel;
It is the space within that makes it useful.
Cut doors and windows for a room;
It is the holes which make it useful.
Therefore profit comes from what is there;
Usefulness from what is not there.

–Verse 11, *Tao Te Ching,* Gia-Fu Feng/Jane English translation

Vibration is mental, spiritual, and also physical. We are electromagnetic beings

Vibration

surrounded by an exterior electromagnetic spectrum that permeates our living spaces via devices, appliances and broadcast waves. Whether the electric grid runs on 60 Hz or 50 Hz, that frequency (plus its overtones) infuses the spaces we occupy, and also enters our bodies. Notice the pitch of the hum of your refrigerator, washing machine, vacuum cleaner, weed wacker, car motor. You'll find–if your electric grid is based on 60 Hz as it is in North America–that the foundational hum of appliances and motors falls somewhere between a B (61.73 Hz in ET) and a B flat (58.27 Hz). Usually overtones of this pitch can be heard as well.

    Part of our job as musicians is to notice frequencies around us. We also need to notice the so-called background music broadcast in buildings, supermarkets, offices and elsewhere. This music is programmed at specific tempos, keys and styles designed to control the mood of the occupants. Additionally, there are often subliminal messages being broadcast on hidden carrier frequencies! These things are all part of the frequency awareness we wish to cultivate as musicians.

The range of human hearing is said to be between 20 Hz and 20,000 Hz. The abbreviation "Hz" stands for Hertz and simply means 'cycles per second.' A tone of 20 Hz is close to an E (20.6 Hz in Equal Temperament) below the lowest A on the piano, but as a sine wave it is generally not audible. You would have to use a wave that generates overtones like a square, triangle or sawtooth in order to hear it.

Nothing is at rest, so even a single sustained tone is vibrating all by itself. Extremely low pitches can no longer be discerned as tones, but only as oscillations. You can actually hear the beats of the frequency because it's vibrating so slowly.

20,000 Hz, on the opposite end of the spectrum, is quite a high pitch and may be inaudible for many people. Just above that is the burglar alarm or dog whistle range. Still, it's good for your headphones and other audio equipment to have the 20 Hz - 20 kHz range in order to enhance the bass and the overtones. Don't buy crappy stuff!

Vibration

You can experiment with these concepts by downloading a free frequency generator app.

The process of tuning two instruments to each other is a representation of the Principle of Vibration in action. When the instruments are not in tune, 'beats' (pulses) are generated. The presence of beats indicates that the frequencies of each instrument are not aligned. When one instrument adjusts to the other so that they are in tune, no beats are heard. But we know we're in tune not so much because we hear it, but because we feel it. (Flute players, or players of any instrument that cannot produce the same volume level as brass or electronic instruments, know this very well. When playing in an ensemble that is overpowering the sound of our own instrument to the point where we can't hear ourselves, we have to tune by feeling. It's similar to a vocalist knowing where the pitch is by the feeling in the vocal cords and the resonant cavities in the upper body.)

One could say that we hear what is there, but we feel what is not there. We hear the note, but we feel the rest. Our efforts to truly understand the Principle of Vibration must include the vibration of what is there, and the vibration of what is not there. Sometimes in conversation a pause says everything. In fact, we even have the expression "pregnant pause" denoting that type of silence.

The Hermetic literature includes a tract from the *Nag Hammadi Library* titled "The Discourse on the Eighth and Ninth," referring to the realms existing beyond the first seven surrounding the earth. From the chapter introduction of the Robinson edition: "*In ancient times it was thought that the first seven spheres were the realms of the sun, moon, and planets, the lower powers whose control over human life was not necessarily benevolent. The eighth and ninth spheres thus designate the beginning of the divine realm, the levels beyond the control of the lower powers. At death the soul would journey through the seven spheres, and after successful passage it would reach the eighth and the ninth, the levels at which the soul could experience true bliss. Furthermore, the eighth and the ninth spheres can also indicate advanced stages of spiritual development.*"

Vibration

Musically speaking, we immediately equate the "lower seven" spheres with the diatonic scale. This correlation would suggest that the 'notes' belong to a more base level of music, whereas the rests, symbolized by the eighth and ninth spheres, denote a more spiritual aspect of music. The tract is a conversation between Hermes Trismegistus and a disciple. Hermes says, *"For the entire eighth, O my son, and the souls that are in it, and the angels, sing a hymn in silence. And I, Mind, understand."* The disciple, however, doesn't get why or how the hymn is silent. Hermes explains, *"I am singing a hymn within myself."*

A unique phenomenon we experience mostly when playing duets is that of difference tones. I first became aware of difference tones (aka combination tones) while playing Telemann flute duets with Jay Brandford in my Brooklyn apartment about 30 years ago. We noticed when we played certain notes the combination would create a 'buzzing' in the ear. Then we heard that this buzzing was actually a very low pitch. The frequency of this pitch equalled the frequency of the higher pitch minus the lower pitch, hence the term 'difference tone.' We started mapping out the pitch combinations that produced this phenomenon, not realizing that Hindemith had already done that in 1942! The first documented report of difference tones actually goes back to 18th century composer Giuseppe Tartini.

The acoustical phenomenon of difference tones was, according to Hindemith, used by pipe organ manufacturers when making smaller instruments. Since these organs could not accommodate the very large pipes, the lowest notes were produced by two small pipes that were both activated by the same key. The resulting difference tone would sound the needed low note.

Just as you have to activate your new credit card before you can use it, you have to activate the vibration of your instrument. That's why we warm up. Few musicians realize the purpose of the warmup. Most believe that the warmup is for them. The reality is that the warmup is for the instrument. Regardless of the material of which it is composed—wood, metal, plastic, carbon fiber, hard rubber, ceramic, etc.–

Vibration

the molecules of that material must be put into vibration mode. They must be 'activated.' We do this by simply playing the instrument (this also applies to the human voice). When the molecules separate more, as they're heated by air or friction, it allows more space for the material to vibrate and the resonance increases.

This is also why a master can play different instruments and produce the same signature tone quality on each. Listen to recordings of legendary jazz innovator Charlie Parker. Because he was often without an instrument, he would play on a variety of borrowed horns, including the white plastic alto saxophone heard on the Jazz at Massey Hall recording. He sounds like himself no matter what horn he plays. Similarly, master pianists exhibit the same sound every time they perform, even though they are playing on the instrument supplied by the venue rather than their personal instrument.

Just as we recognize the voice of people we know well, music cognoscenti recognize great players by their sound. This is especially apparent on an instrument like the saxophone which supports a wide range of overtones. Different players produce different tonal characteristics because of their focus on certain harmonics and waveforms. This is not a conscious process. One's signature tone is acquired through externalizing the tone one hears in one's head, and that process belongs to the subconscious mind. We train the process with conscious thoughts/actions which, through repetition, become subconscious.

One's individual sound is produced from within the player, regardless of whether the instrument is of the wind, string or percussion family.

The ear works by converting sound waves into electrical signals that pass through to the brain, where they are interpreted. But to think that perceiving the vibrations of music depends only on the ear would be incorrect. We can actually perceive vibrations with our entire body, or parts of it like fingers and feet. This is how it's possible for a deaf musician, like the Grammy winning percussionist Evelyn Glennie, to perform at the highest level. She explains that as a young girl she was fortunate to have a

Vibration

teacher with the patience to train her how to feel the frequencies for different notes.

A hearing musician does the same thing, perhaps without realizing it. I myself have had many playing experiences when I couldn't hear myself due to the volume level of the surrounding instruments, particularly while playing flute. If you can't hear yourself, how do you know you're playing in tune? Answer: by feeling the vibration. When it's in tune, it feels right. Hindemith goes into great detail, in Book I of *The Craft of Musical Composition*, on the purpose of the difference tones (he calls them 'combination tones'). He emphasizes that they allow the player to achieve accurate intonation by having that 'support tone' way down low as the foundation. That support tone–the difference tone/combination tone–is usually not heard. But it is felt. Just as we don't normally notice the foundation of a house, yet that foundation is supporting the entire structure above it.

We need to feel the vibrations of our own instrument, and the instruments we're playing with. We can easily be distracted from feeling, however, especially when the volume level is high. Indeed, when I'm at the sound check I always go out front and block my ears while listening to the levels. That means I'm blocking part of the sound spectrum (particularly the highs) and I can hear the blend of the instruments much better, so I know which instrument needs to come down in the mix.

Perceiving the vibration of musical space is just as important as perceiving the vibration of sound. I'm referring to the vibration of the resonance and/or silence between the notes. The Japanese refer to this space as *ma*. The *ma* is the sound before it's born, and after it dies. Incorporating the *ma* means we can express the entire life of a sound, as in the striking of a bell. The sound exists from before the bell is struck, through the strike, through the gradual decay of the sound, and finally to the fading out of the sound and the ensuing silence. We can then experience the journey of the sound from before it happens all the way through to the memory it leaves behind.

Think of the opening measures of Beethoven's Symphony No. 5. When I was young I thought the familiar opening figure was a triplet starting on the downbeat. Later on, when I had the chance to play the piece in an orchestra, I saw the music for the first time. It's not a triplet and it doesn't start with a note, it starts with a rest. (Of course it starts with a rest–Beethoven was hip–he would never start that figure on a downbeat).

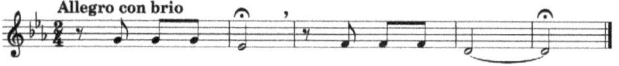

If you've ever spent time on top of a mountain, you know the feeling of *ma*. There is a vibration there, but it's one of silence. It has weight. *Ma* is what we have with musical rests. The rests have a weight to them, which is why, as young musicians, we were told they were "notes of silence." If it weren't for the vibration of the rests, the notes would have no meaning. That's why I always say we don't play the notes, we play the rests.

Anyone can play notes. A master plays the rests.

Reader comments

George Neidorf: One evening, at the end of a set, a bass playing friend said that when he was outside he knew it was me playing because of the sound. I was playing someone else's drums and hadn't retuned them. At that time I wasn't aware that I had my own sound and had no idea how I produced it. Eventually, I knew it was who I was, and how I struck the drum, that produced a discernible sound.

Nina Ott: I'm reminded of seeing Jaki Byard play several times on really poor pianos and getting his own, beautiful, very unique sound - every time! Oh my! I couldn't believe it. As far as rests, silence, space: this is a big one for me lately. Waiting for the next idea with love and trust. Something about letting go, something about that works for me.

Marco Romano: "Rests" reminded me of some famous musician (Ellington?) who said what you do not play is as important as what you play.

HERMETIC PRINCIPLE 4: POLARITY

"...everything must be the product of opposition and contrariety, and it cannot be otherwise."
–Corpus Hermeticum

The fourth Hermetic Principle is Polarity. It states there are always two poles to any subject, and all the subject's manifestations are connected by those two poles. The difference between these seemingly opposing poles is only a matter of degree. As an example let's look at Hot and Cold. In one sense they aren't opposing conditions. Hot and cold both concern temperature therefore they belong to the same scale or plane. Cold is merely the absence of heat. The difference between them is the degree, or the position of each on the same plane of Heat.

Light and Dark: Dark is not an opposing force to light, it's just the absence of light. We can be blinded by too much light as well as the lack of light.

Stillness and Motion: A moving object can go so fast that it appears to be still (think of the spokes of a rotating wheel). Conversely, a still object can be perceived as being in motion, like the rapidly sequenced frames in a 'motion picture' or a flip book.

Sound and Silence: In the Vibration chapter we spoke about the silence found at the top of a mountain. There may be no other sounds, but the silence itself is a sound. Deaf percussionist Evelyn Glennie says "Silence is the loudest, heaviest sound to experience." Silence has weight, just like rests in music.

Among other laws, the Taoist taiji symbol, commonly called the 'yin-yang' symbol, expresses the law of polarity. At the fullest point

Polarity

of the yang we see a small dot of yin, and vice versa. We want to be able to play with these polarities, not be imprisoned by them.

"Nature attains productivity by means of polarity... truth is often crucified between the two thieves of apparent contradiction." Manly P. Hall, *The Secret Teachings of All Ages*

I thought of a funny idea for a T shirt:
YIN IS THE NEW YANG

The absurdity of this statement is surely on a par with another T shirt I have that says "Matriarchy Now!" I wear the shirt as a joke, because the extreme of the matriarchy pole is just as imbalanced as that of the patriarchy pole. No, grasshopper, says the Master, the point of polarity is to play with it, not go to one pole and stay there. Even our Earth reverses its poles with relative regularity!

Ultimately, polarity is an illusion, but a necessary one. Duality is part of the human condition. The Principle of Polarity explores duality relationships and gives us a way to unify the seemingly opposing poles when we know the big picture. Moreover, polarity allows us, as humans, to experience the full range of emotions and impressions available to us. A loud note enables us to play a soft note, and vice versa.

Peter J. Carroll, in his book *Liber Null*, says "the wise seek satisfaction in that which repels as well as that which attracts."

Polarity

Contemplation of his examples can lead to a great deal of insight:
- Sex - Death
- Release - Dissolution
- Atrophy - Frustration
- Fear - Desire
- Terror - Joy
- Fright - Attraction
- Aversion - Greed
- Hate - Love
- Anger - Rapture
- Aggression - Passion
- Loathing - Attachment
- Elation - Depression
- Pleasure - Pain
- Laughter - Laughter (it is its own opposite!)

We need these polarities in order to have a complete experience of life. Theodore Roosevelt, in his book *Strenuous Life*, expressed it thus:

"Far better it is to dare mighty things, to win glorious triumphs, even though checkered

by failure, than to take rank with those poor spirits who neither enjoy much nor suffer much, because they live in the gray twilight that knows neither victory nor defeat."

One actively uses the Principle of Polarity when jumping: in order to go up, we first crouch down. In a foot race, one pushes against the ground behind in order to move forward.

The popular expression "go with the flow" is the idea of moving along the spectrum of polarity and not getting stuck in one position. We can advance toward one pole or the other, go back and correct something, keep going in the same direction, or change directions at any time.

There is an even more sophisticated understanding of polarity, and that is to see not only the unification of the poles on a single plane, but also that each point on the plane has its own polarity within itself!

"Alternating the force of pulling and pushing severs an opponent's root

*so that he can be defeated
quickly and certainly.
Full and empty
should be clearly differentiated.
At any place where there is emptiness,
there must be fullness;
Every place has both emptiness and fullness."*
— *The Tai Chi Classics*

Polarity is also expressed in the inversions of intervals. A minor second inverted becomes a major seventh. A major second inverted becomes a minor seventh. A minor third inverted becomes a major sixth, and a major third becomes a minor sixth. Small leaps, inverted, become large, and vice versa. Minor intervals inverted become major, and vice versa.

A professional performer must create the passion that communicates to the audience, while remaining in control of the performance. Maintaining control is part and parcel of professionalism, and separates the pros from the amateurs.

Years ago I was attending a reading of Hafez, the Persian spiritual poet. The poems were being read by the man who translated them, and at one point he became so moved by the poetry that he began to cry–in the middle of the reading! (Apparently he didn't have experience as a performer, only as a translator.)

As a professional musician with decades of experience, watching this scenario solidified for me the importance of maintaining the two poles while performing. On the one hand, you have to immerse a part of Self in the feeling. But then you have to back off and just simulate the feeling, so it can be controlled within the setting you find yourself. You have to objectify the feeling. For performers this is mandatory. If you're an actor, you have to recreate the character's feelings while not forgetting your lines and your stage directions. Likewise, musicians have to communicate the emotion of the music, but not lose our place and our role in the music at any given moment.

I liken it to being a designated driver. While other parts of self are crying or laughing,

Polarity

the driver-self takes it all in but doesn't become consumed by it.

I have heard certain show biz personalities say: "It's all about sincerity. Once you can fake that, you've got it made!"

Of course, we're not faking anything when we play. Speaking for myself and most of my colleagues, we give everything we've got to each performance. Yet we simultaneously hold the big picture of the music being played, our role in creating that music, the interaction with the ensemble, the audience, practical things such as our distance from the microphone, and other factors.

"You own the room, or the room owns you." – Bobby Short

Ultimately we want balance; but balance isn't achieved by picking a spot in the middle and staying there. That's not possible to do, because all relationships are in a constant state of flux. So true balance means being sensitive to the flow of energy and moving in accordance with it. Understanding the Principle of Polarity means we can slide along and change something in the direction of the opposite pole, anytime we want.

This is why we can easily use the diatonic scale or the pentatonic scale to improvise. The lower octave of the scale can be thought of as the negative pole ('negative' in terms of 'yin') and the upper octave can be considered the positive, 'yang' pole. As we move to different parts of the scale in our improvisation, we move to different positions in the scale's polarity. That gives a nice sense of movement to our creation.

If you want to experiment with this idea, find a *shruti* box drone you can play or sing along with. (There are *shruti* apps, or you can find a recording online.) Of course, you don't have to limit yourself to the diatonic or pentatonic scale since the drone is just a fifth; feel free to try out different modes that use the minor 3rd, the minor 7th, the flat 5, or other alterations. The objective is to get a feel for the movement toward each pole–that is, the lower or upper octave.

Polarity

Everyone knows that the basic tonal polarity of music is major vs minor. There is only one degree that determines whether the scale or chord is major or minor, that being the third. Yet there is no objective point at which we can say a minor third becomes a major third. The ear only knows this by context. Paul Hindemith, in his book *The Craft of Musical Composition*, even uses Hermetic terms when describing the 'difference' between minor and major thirds! Note also that he recognizes the truth that the two poles of a polarity relationship are not separate things. The polarity is a relationship between positions in a whole.

"Since one cannot even say definitely where the minor third leaves off and the major third begins, I do not believe in any polarity of the two chords. They are the high and low, the strong and weak, the light and dark, the bright and dull forms of the same sound. It is true that the overtone series contains both forms of the third (4:5 and 5:6) in pure form, but that does not alter the fact that the boundary between them is vague. Pure thirds furnish us with pure forms of

both major and minor triads. But the ear allows within the triads, too, a certain latitude to the thirds, so that on one and the same root a number of major triads and a number of minor triads can be erected, no two alike in the exact size of their thirds. Triads in which the third lies in the indeterminate middle ground can, like the third itself, be interpreted as major or minor, according to the context. But why the almost negligible distance between the major and minor thirds should have such extraordinary psychological significance remains a mystery."
—Paul Hindemith, *The Craft of Musical Composition*

If you examine older editions of classical pieces, you'll see that the dynamic range extends from *pppp* to *ffff*. Yet in modern editions we rarely see these extremes of dynamics. The most we'll see is *ppp/fff*, or maybe only *pp/ff*. This is a shame because it is certainly possible to express each pole of dynamic level as well as each point on its spectrum. Perhaps it's a result of the raising of volume levels and dependence on electronics in the current era. Regardless,

Polarity

music is supposed to have these polarities of dynamics and good musicians should be able to play them.

Another aspect of Polarity that we use not only in music but also in all the arts, is the concept "Tension and Release." Good art has elements of tension (as in tonal dissonance or an *ostinato*) and it has release (as in resolving cadences or going from a pedal point to a walking bass).

We also deal with polarity when programming sets or concerts. Knowing how to sequence the repertoire is a hard-won skill. We want to vary tempos, time signatures, grooves, tonalities, and we want our set to reflect the entire spectrum of polarities. (And just like a good quarterback, we have to be able to 'call an audible' on the fly, rearranging the sequence when the vibe calls for it.)

In the original days of recording, an agonizing amount of thought was put into the order of the songs. Now that people download individual songs and make playlists out of them, the order of the songs on an album doesn't seem as important–but musicians still put the same amount of time into it because we tend to conceive an album as a set of music, an entirety in itself.

In sports, the movement of teams on the field doesn't stay in one direction. It changes when the other team gets the ball and starts moving toward the opposing team's goal, to the point that we can't be sure who will win the game. This is the wonderful aspect of play that is so engaging; a close game is much more fun to watch than one where the teams are clearly unequal.

Composers, too, play with the concept of "it ain't over till it's over." We even have a type of cadence called the 'deceptive cadence' that fools the listener into expecting a resolution to a I chord after a V chord, but goes to another chord instead.

When we find ourselves at the extreme of a polarity, we know that we will never be at an extreme for very long. Universe is based on change, and even though it doesn't always appear that way, we're always moving from one place on the spectrum to another place. Speaking abstractly, it's a relief to realize that certain doom may be averted, and sobering to know that the yellow brick road may have unforeseen detours. As the popular slogan goes, "it's all about the journey."

Finally, we always look for the polarity between inner and outer expression. Inner expression refers not only to the way we're processing our emotions, but also to the workings of the subconscious mind of which we're not consciously aware. When creating, the outer expression must be informed by the inner aspect in order for the art to have integrity.

We want to use the principle of polarity, in all its musical aspects, to play the game of Music. It's a fun game. And we are very, very serious about it.

Reader comments

Mark Ax: There is so much fear of polarity of late. But the real fear should be the lack of relation between the poles.

Alki Steriopoulos: The necessity of a pendulum swinging to extremes. It is only thus that the middle ground is discovered. Polarities and all the points between, form a line of continuity. As in music, in life.

Susan Hart: The principle is similar in creating good visual art. Without opposition and contrariety, there is no dynamic.

Bud Revels: One of our arranging teachers at MSM used to use the philosophy of "Aesthetic Realism" liberally in examining great arrangements or film scores. One of the primary principles is "Aesthetic Realism, in keeping with its name, sees all reality including the reality that is oneself, as the aesthetic oneness of opposites."

HERMETIC PRINCIPLE 5:
RHYTHM

"...in everything there is manifested a measured motion; a to-and-from movement; a flow and inflow; a swing forward and backward; a pendulum-like movement; a tide-like ebb and flow; a high-tide and a low-tide...there is no such thing as absolute rest, or cessation from movement, and all movement partakes of Rhythm."
—The Kybalion

The 5th Hermetic principle is that of Rhythm. We can see how closely the Principle of Rhythm is to that of Polarity. Between Polarity's two poles, we experience the fluctuation and flow of rhythm. But rhythm doesn't go to the extremes of the poles. It stays more in the middle, establishing a pulse within a close range. The other aspect that distinguishes rhythm from polarity is its use of stressed and unstressed elements, and syncopation.

In music we draw far more rhythmic patterns from nature than we may realize. The bossa nova bass drum pattern, for instance, comes from the human heartbeat. How many other correspondences might we be able to find if we start noticing them?

I'm not in the habit of frequenting dance clubs (but I did go to Area in NYC a bunch of times back in the day when my friend JB was the bartender) not only because as I've matured I dislike crowds, but also because the music is so loud. The volume level of almost every type of performance has raised significantly over the years. My personal theory is that most people's lives are filled with the artificial accoutrements of modern society, and they've lost touch with the life-sustaining rhythms of Nature. They seek to replace those rhythms artificially, with loud music (especially bass) that permeates the body with its vibrations. For many people, this is

Rhythm

as close to a metaphysical experience as they're ever going to get.

In writing and in speech we indicate rhythm not just with the words chosen, but also with punctuation. In music we have rests and phrasing. In dance we have pauses and suspensions. In visual art we have gradations and interruptions of line and shape. There is this idea of rhythm as a continuous thing, yet that continuity includes the spaces that surround and define the other elements.

It's funny that students seem to be very limited when trying to create rhythms, because it's all around us in spoken language. One of my favorite improvisation exercises is to take a poem and put notes to it, using one note for each syllable. (This is a bit different from songwriting, where we often stretch a syllable out over two or more notes.) For best results, use a good poem! Even if you don't have any poetry books, there is no end of wonderful material on the internet, for free.

When I'm teaching students how to play jazz I use the bebop style as a base. The lyrical challenge of choosing certain notes in the chord to connect with other notes in the following chord, and so on, while stressing some and ghosting others, actually mimics the rhythm of the English language. (That's not surprising given that bebop was invented in the U.S. by American musicians.) In fact, the delicious rhythmic motifs of the English language can be used to create other kinds of music as well. (It would be an interesting study to analyze how different languages may have influenced the development of the musical culture in any given country.)

In daily life we can observe the rhythmic changing of moods, how the body feels, phases of hunger or fulfillment of desires, negative or positive mental states. The Hermeticists use this principle to realize how easily we fall into a rhythm and in fact are controlled by it. The aim, therefore, is to acknowledge the natural principle of Rhythm and so utilize it for one's benefit by "riding" it skillfully.

Along these lines, I've always wondered what people mean by 'happiness.' To me, happiness is not a condition, but rather a series of moments that can be interrupted at any time.

Rhythm

If I observe myself and notice that I feel happy, it's only a matter of time before another emotion will supersede the happy feeling. This is rhythm in action. There are no permanent conditions, everything is in constant change, constant flow. In the 60s people said "go with the flow," meaning it was better to time one's actions to the rhythm of surrounding conditions rather than fight the conditions. Yet anyone who's studied martial arts knows the flow can also be guided to flow differently! So the flow is not necessarily something to submit to; rather, it's something to perceive and internalize, then guide from inside it. You have to know where the flow is before you can go with it or guide it.

Every musician has had the experience of starting a song in one tempo, and by the end finding it has slowed down or sped up, sometimes considerably. When we come to a difficult passage in a piece we're practicing, we often slow down; when we know a passage or an exercise really well, we tend to speed up.

This is being controlled by the force of Rhythm. Because rhythm has its own pulse, it can carry us away from our intended course, just like the current of a river. The main tool we use to train control of this force is the metronome. The metronome keeps us honest with the time, so that we can learn to differentiate between an unconscious subjection to the rhythm and a conscious, involved relationship with it.

Think of it like sledding down a hill in the snow, or going down a steep hill on a bicycle. We are propelled by the conditions, but we must maintain control or we'll wipe out.

That said, in some cases it can be acceptable for a tempo to increase, as long as it is a natural result of the intensity of the music. But in general you don't want a slow tempo to get even slower.

The tendency of bright tempos is to increase, while the tendency of slow tempos is to drag.

The Hermeticists also look on all the principles as manifesting not only in one lifetime, but rather over the course of the entire existence of the spirit. Because music is always

Rhythm

a microcosm of Life in some way, we can use the art of programming as an example of the Principle of Rhythm. When we're making a set list for a gig, or a concert program, we're thinking of groove, rhythm and tempo as the prime differentiators for the pieces. (A secondary factor is tonality, like whether the piece is major or minor, and in what key. We usually don't want to play two pieces in a row that are in the same key.)

We may open with something exciting, with a faster tempo or engaging groove. Then something slower. A waltz in there somewhere. A 5/4 or 7/4 piece. A medium groove, a ballad. We often close a set or a performance with another exciting piece, which could be a faster tempo or perhaps a stimulating Latin or Afro-Cuban groove. (I'm speaking here of a jazz set. Other genres will have their own specific requirements, but the programming nevertheless follows a sequence containing, primarily, rhythmic variation.)

Jazz musicians know a lot about rhythm, but they don't know as much as Indian musicians. One time a jazz drummer got a gig with an Indian band. He showed up to the gig and said to the sitar player, "hey man, I've never played Indian music before, can you give me any tips before we start?" The Indian musician says "It's easy! Just play a heavy backbeat on 5 and 13 and you'll be fine."

Many songs are actually more recognized by their rhythm than their notes. Can you identify any of the following songs only from their rhythm? (Answers at the end of the chapter.)

Rhythm

Fig. 1
Allegro

Fig. 2
Lento
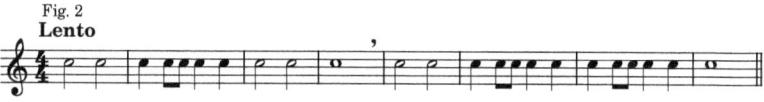

Fig. 3
Andante

Fig. 4
Allegro con brio

Rhythm doesn't belong only to music; it's a universal principle in all the arts, as well as in Nature. Phrases such as "the rhythm of life...the rhythm of the tides...there's rhythm in her movements...try to disrupt your opponent's rhythm....he couldn't find his rhythm" are commonplace. The rhythm is what keeps our attention, sometimes to the point of entrancement.

Rhythmic force first must be perceived, then felt in the body. Once we can do that, we have the power to either fit into the rhythm or change it, whichever is more appropriate.

When I was 12 years old and learning how to improvise, my parents took me to a Milt Hinton concert at the bandshell in Westport, CT. After the concert I approached the stage to say to Mr. Hinton that I enjoyed the concert, and by the way, how do you improvise? Do you know that man invited me onto the stage and gave me a lesson at the piano for 20 minutes! I'll never forget that he told me the most important thing in your solo is the rhythm.

A popular lifestyle term is 'biorhythm,' referring to the physical (23 days), emotional

(28 days) and mental (33 days) cycles of human beings. This is different from the biological rhythms (like 'circadian rhythm') described in scientific circles. There have been some fascinating experiments with biological rhythms involving people living underground for extended periods, without natural light, or in miniature biospheres like enclosed glass domes. My friend John DiLeva Halpern conceived just such a project many years ago. He was the human subject in a glass installation filled with plants, containing everything he would need to survive for ten days.

He told me the first day in the glass structure with the plants he was surrounded by onlookers gazing at him through the glass. Upon nightfall, since he had no artificial lighting, the onlookers dispersed and he got ready for bed. He awoke in the middle of the night in a panic, unable to breathe! He suddenly realized that the plants had taken all the oxygen and were now in their rhythmic night cycle of dispersing carbon dioxide. Without any means of communication to the outside world, John, an experienced meditator, used his spiritual practice to calm himself in order to use as little of the remaining oxygen as possible. Rhythm to the rescue: at sunrise the plants began their day cycle, once again infusing the structure with oxygen. As the experiment progressed, the oxygen output of the plants increased and the nighttime cycle gradually contained more oxygen.

Perhaps of all the Hermetic principles, Rhythm is the one most closely aligned to our sense of being alive. The rhythmic pulsing of one's heartbeat and respiration is always there, in the background, connecting us to the rhythms and cycles of our planet.

When we understand the Hermetic principle of Rhythm we can find our place in the world, and in the universe. Maybe all this is what Gloria Estefan was trying to tell us. . .

Rhythm

Reader comments

Alki Steriopoulos: Living in NYC I remember hours and days delighting in the constant music available everywhere. You'll never hear anything funkier than the rhythmic counterpoint of a subway car, no, *several* subway cars, rolling over the tracks, dopplering in and out of sync, while the orchestration of sirens, traffic, human cries of laughter, despair, and conversation, all float in and out of earshot, making a constant that, like a river, could never be stepped in twice. Even the smells were part of the soundscape. Joni Mitchell called it the "sweet cacophony of New York City." And all of it for free. All you had to "pay" was attention.

Marco Romano: The cadence of the patois of Guadeloupe is based on 7 drum rhythms.

Answers to rhythms:

Fig. 1 = Happy Birthday
Fig. 2 = Over the Rainbow
Fig. 3 = Yesterday
Fig. 4 = Allegro movement, Beethoven's Fifth Symphony

Music and the 7 Hermetic Principles

HERMETIC PRINCIPLE 6:
CAUSE & EFFECT

"The Masters obey the Causation of the higher planes, but they help to RULE on their own plane."
–The Kybalion

Of all the Hermetic Principles, the Law of Cause and Effect seems the most obvious. Few would argue with the idea that every effect has a cause, and so on into retrograde infinity. The opposite is also true, that every cause has an effect. We reap what we sow (if we plant arugula seeds we ain't gonna get zucchini) is another way of putting it.

But what if it's not obvious? Often we see an effect for which we don't know the cause, and often a cause doesn't produce the expected effect. We have many influences that play out on a subconscious level, for instance.

"Everything we see is caused by something or else it could not exist. We live in a world of effects. The phenomenal world, the world as seen, with all its differently shaped and coloured objects, is a world of effects. The causes of these effects are not visible. They lie behind the effects. They are not immediately evident to the senses. But they may become so to the mind. The connection between cause and effect is a mystery, because cause and effect are on different levels.

"Now it is clear that it is necessary to think concerning the cause of a thing–that is, to use the mind. For example, in a detective story, there is a dead body. This is an effect evident to the senses. But the cause is not evident in the same way. Only the use of the mind will reveal it. That is, the plane or level of causes is different from the effects produced by them. and

Cause & Effect

here, of course, endless errors thrive and flourish, because effects can be attributed to the wrong cause. Now if we could think from right causes we would move in the direction of more interior thought, which sees more. In one effect there are many causes. When we take ourselves as one being, we think from effect, from appearance. When we realize that we are many different beings, we begin to think from the level of causes. In short, we begin to think more interiorly and so, instead of seeing one being, we see many beings." –Maurice Nicoll, *Commentaries*, Vol. 4, p. 1484

The law of Cause and Effect is often thought of in relation to Isaac Newton's Third Law of Motion: for every action there is an equal and opposite reaction. Newton's work is considered representative of the beginning of the Age of Enlightenment in Europe (although why it's called the Age of Enlightenment is a mystery, because surely most of the Ascended Masters and others who are actually enlightened would disagree with most of its tenets). At first glance it seems there is a sequence: action, then reaction. Time unfolding, from the past to the future. Yet if we examine this law more closely, we see that it doesn't say "there will be an equal and opposite reaction." Rather, it says "there *is* an equal and opposite reaction." The action/reaction described by Newton occurs at the same time. As you take a step, putting your weight on the earth, the earth pushes against you simultaneously. The force and the body executing it are joined, but are separate things. So it's not that an action is followed by a reaction; it's that the force generated cannot exist without its pair–the reactive force that is its equal and opposite.

Enough physics…for now!

When we approach the Principle of Cause and Effect with our 'daily life mind' we put it on a trajectory that unfolds in Time. Everything that happens we see as having been caused by something that happened prior to that. Yet this notion of Time as an arrow is unique to the Western mind. Good lord, Western thought is married to linear time as if sanctified by the Church itself. Yet the view held by Eastern sages is that Time is not a linear phenomenon but a cyclical phenomenon. Western esoteric thought has gradually come 'round to the same view. In other words, it is only our limitation as human beings that forces a perception of Time as sequential rather than cyclical–or even simultaneous, with everything happening all at once, which is what the really enlightened beings tell us!

The 2022 film *Everything Everywhere All At Once* explores the latter theme. The protagonist, a Chinese-American woman struggling with family and economic issues and an IRS audit, at the moments of highest stress finds herself jumping into other selves and other timelines. In order to navigate her 'current' life, she must learn from mistakes she makes in other lives (and other dimensions), while also drawing on powers she has in other lives/dimensions but lacks in the 'current' one.

Readers were introduced to the same idea with the 1969 publication of Kurt Vonnegut's novel *Slaughterhouse Five*. The protagonist, Billy Pilgrim, becomes "unstuck in Time" and at random moments finds himself in the bombing of Dresden during World War II, or in a plane crash in Vermont, or held prisoner in a geodesic dome cage on the planet of Tralfamadore.

It turns out the key to understanding why the Law of Cause and Effect is so incredibly profound is in letting go of the Time-is-an-arrow idea and realizing that everything operates on multiple dimensions, most of which are imperceptible to us even as they influence the three dimensions we know and love. To get more into the idea, let's take the concept of Karma. Contrary to popular thought, karma (which is more or less cosmic retribution for one's deeds, particularly the evil ones) isn't necessarily something that plays out the following week, month or year, or even in one lifetime. We see evidence of this everywhere: all the creeps who seemingly have a great life, and all the good folks who get shafted!

As soon as we let go of the idea that karma is encapsulated into a single lifetime, it starts to make sense. There's a cool series by yet another Newton: Master Hypnotherapist Dr. Michael Newton's books contain case studies of patients who entered into states of being that were actually between lifetimes. This was very helpful for them because they were able to see how their karma played out over the course of two or more incarnations. Newton's findings are meticulously researched. He wrote his books based on his work with over 7000 patients, and waited 25 years before publishing.

By the way, even if you don't believe in something like reincarnation, the truth is we really don't know for sure. Unless we do. Because there are people that can perceive other dimensions. Some of them even do it without any drugs!

You may be a skeptic by nature. I hear you. I'd like to believe someone who tells me they can see ghosts or communicate with crystals, even though I can't do that. But then I realize the stuff musicians do every day is also seen as miraculous by those who can't do it.

We can take Cause and Effect literally, on the physical plane of daily existence. Yet just as with the concept of karma, we can realize this principle operates on planes and levels far beyond the physical, quotidian experience of

Life. The 20th century mystic Gurdjieff, for example, spoke of the Law of Octaves. He said that as one develops one's soul and one's capacity for perception beyond the merely physical, one is subject to fewer of the so-called 'natural laws.'

Another meaning of the Hermetic Principle of Cause and Effect is that nothing "merely happens." There's no such thing as chance. Yet energy can be guided toward certain outcomes, and this is as true on the physical plane as on any other. For example: someone who has a strong desire to visit another country might start by viewing photographs of the country, checking on flights, even learning some of the language. In that way, energy is established which enhances the goal. It's like a siphon—the first thing you have to do is get the flow started from your end, then it will move on its own.

We have the impression that Time is continuous. Scientists are now leaning towards 'packets' (or frames) of Time, just like a movie ("motion picture"). It may be that our brain creates the illusion of continuous time in order to make our lives smoother. There are many available experiences which bear out the 'frames of time' scenario: meditation, DMT, traumatic episodes, ayahuasca or psilocybin or LSD, trance/hypnotic states, spontaneous perceptions like deja vu, dream states, and more. One night on an ayahuasca journey I looked at my watch and it was midnight. I waited an hour and looked at my watch again. It was 12:05. (As a result, the wristwatch went into a drawer and didn't come out for 13 years, 5 months and 29 days...sorry I don't know the time, by then the watch had stopped running.)

Likewise, we tend to think of music as something that unfolds in Time in a linear fashion. Thematic material from the beginning of the piece is echoed, embellished or compositionally altered as the piece develops. Jazz, however, might be thought of as more cyclical, since its traditional form repeats the initial harmonic structure continually in a series of 'choruses.'

There is a further way to relate Music to Time, and that's by examining music's horizontal aspect vs. its vertical aspect. What does this mean? We normally experience music sequentially: one measure, the next measure, etc. This is what I would call the horizontal aspect, and it's the one we're most familiar with. Yet there is another aspect, and that is the "vertical" perception of music, or rather, of a sound. Musically speaking that sound can be either a single note or a chord. In the opening scene of Peter Brook's film *Meetings With Remarkable Men*, we see a musician who can make the mountains resonate with the sound of his voice, even though the other musicians can't. This is using the vertical understanding. The purity of tone quality, the depth of feeling, the gravity of musical wisdom, the connection between Earth, Human, Heaven–these things are what's expressed in a vertical perception of sound. Additionally, we can apply this to complex music that unfolds in Time, but also can be isolated at any moment to zoom in on the vertical aspect.

Fledgling jazz improvisors are told they should "tell a story" with their improvised solo. And they should. Because they're just starting out and they need to learn that. Once the narrative function of music is mastered, an advanced musician can begin exploring the reality contained in the vertical perception. That involves breaking down one sound into its components, which include overtones or harmonics, virtual and spectral pitches, (see my book *Practice Like The Pros*) textures, timbre and alterations of timbre, volume, intensity, and so forth. So you can see that music is far more than just an unfolding of melodic, harmonic and rhythmic sequences–there's a whole Universe in there!

Science refers to Time as the 4th dimension. But don't be one-dimensional and stop there! Just as 3rd dimension beings lord it over the Flatlanders of the 2nd dimension, surely beings of higher dimensions are looking at our concept of Time and laughing themselves silly. But even if we can't control the Time dimension with our physical body, we can and do control it with our mind. There are also physical ways to "play" with dimensions, such as in 2D figures like Penrose Stairs which go endlessly up/down (see below), the illusions of Escher, or *trompe l'oeil* art.

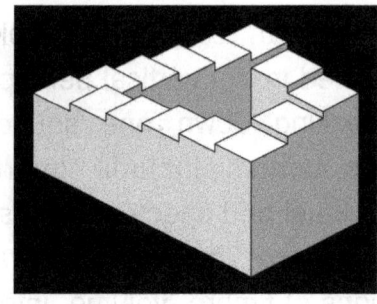

We can liken the 'vertical' aspect of music to the idea of Time being simultaneous. Let's take a musician like John Coltrane. In his later career, he became famous for a technique the critics called "sheets of sound." In this technique the rapid cascade of tones is heard more as a texture than as a sequence of notes. "Texture," like tone, is a quality belonging to the vertical perception of sound.

My perception of Coltrane's later music is that it had a holographic quality that made it multi-dimensional. As such, it wasn't dependent only on unfolding in Time, it also depended on the vertical structure he was creating. I have heard colleagues describe the feeling of hearing this music, and they say you felt "the whole room was elevated" and similar phrases. My description of Coltrane's music as being on both a horizontal and a vertical plane I think would appeal to him, as it echoes the form of the cross and he was a highly religious man. (In fact, after his death he was acknowledged as a saint when the Church of John Coltrane in San Francisco was established.)

I used to play with the extraordinary trumpeter Lew Soloff (1944-2015) quite often in New York. Once he took a solo chorus on a blues that consisted of only one note (a flat 5) in various gradations of tone quality. I commented on it to him afterwards; "*yeah*," he said, "*sometimes I'm just going for texture.*"

The vertical expression of a sound doesn't depend at all on a developing story. In fact, it's almost experienced independently from the story. It is another dimension of Cause and Effect. Hence the attraction for a genre such as Minimalism, which is sometimes criticized as being "repetitive." I'd like to share with you Philip Glass' counter to this criticism, which I heard from him personally some years ago in New York. It was a brilliant exposition that expressed the inner, hidden aspects of Cause and Effect.

Philip first said that there's no such thing as repetition. He made a comparison with breathing. As any meditator knows, each breath we take is unique. Even so, its form is dependent on the previous breath. Likewise the subsequent breath, and so forth. Even though we group these individual breaths together in the act of respiration, each breath has its own quality. Neither is there any guarantee that another breath will follow the present one! Then he came to the bridge: Even though a note may seem to be the same as the one preceding it, he said, it's actually not. The present note is affected by what has come before it. Has the note already been played twice, or five times, or ten times? Every so-called repetition of the note changes the feeling of the note, therefore our experience also changes.

Expounding on Philip's wisdom, I will add the fact that if a real musician (not AI) is playing it, the body, mind and spirit of the player is also altering in each moment, affecting the sound. Another factor is the acoustics in the room. The room's reverb, absorption, standing waves, permeability of the outside, movements of people in the room, and the sound waves themselves, all cause changes in the perception of the music from moment to moment.

One of the most famous minimalist pieces is Terry Riley's In C. When you listen to it (and it's played differently every time because the phrases are modules that are assembled by the ensemble, which also changes) it's possible to be almost unaware of how the piece gets from one point to another. It takes careful listening to follow the development. The slow pace of the development also allows the listener to experience the music on both the horizontal and vertical planes.

Renowned physicist David Bohm's theory of the Implicate Order addresses the issue of repetition in Nature. He says that "each moment is a projection of the whole" but is then re-absorbed by the whole, which affects the next projection of the whole. It can be thought of in terms of ocean waves. Each wave is projected by the whole ocean, but is then re-absorbed into the ocean; the following wave has thus been affected by that re-absorption. The cycle continues indefinitely.

An average listener's perception is very coarse and literally jumps from musical frame to musical frame, unable to maintain focus on the development of the piece. They notice the peaks and valleys, the volume changes, when the chorus comes in, the ending of one song and the beginning of another...but that's only if they're not in the middle of ordering another glass of wine. Compound this sort of superficial perception with the fact that most people listen with their eyes. If there's not a visual element to accompany the music, their attention flies away at the drop of a hi-hat.

For the attentive listener, however, the world of music holds untold treasures. It is mental and spiritual nourishment as well as emotional nourishment. Sometimes we need a song more than we need food. Humans need the elements of rhythm, melody, cadence and narrative, all of which are conveniently provided by Music in a one-stop-shop package. This fact is not lost on those who delight in controlling the masses, as it's much more effective to control people with songs instead of guns. Musical discretion is always advised–as in the case of the *Gates of Hades* YouTube listener who commented *"well that was 9:34 that i will never get back."*

When contemplating the different levels of causes that can create the same effect, I always think of P.D. Ouspensky's short novel *The Strange Life of Ivan Osokin*. Ivan's life is a complete mess: he's lost his job, he's broke, his girlfriend dumped him, etc. He meets a magician who says he can transport Ivan back to childhood, where he will retain all his current memory and he won't have to repeat his past mistakes. Ivan takes him up on it and goes back to when it all started: when he was 12 he threw a spitball in school and got expelled. But when the spitball moment arrives, even though Ivan knows he'll get thrown out of school if he throws it, he throws it anyway. In fact, all the subsequent pivotal moments in Ivan's life end up happening the exact same way.

The point is that Ivan, like most people, doesn't act from a conscious perspective, but rather from the automatic programs of his subconscious mind. Therefore the effects produced in his life will be the same even if the causes are different.

In music we find ourselves on the same trepidatious path: we practice automatically, we listen automatically, and we often play automatically. (Please note I'm *not* speaking here about technique, which must be automated—only in that way can we truly play consciously and creatively. We can't be conscious and creative if we're struggling with technique. This same principle applies to any skill.)

So in order to be effective in our music, we have to think not only about Time's linear construct, but also about music's expression on all levels and in all dimensions.

The division of physics known as String Theory says there are at least 11 dimensions, and maybe as many as 26. But that's nothing compared to Vedic philosophy which dates to the 15th century BCE –these Sanskrit texts speak of no less than 64 dimensions.

From our limited 3D perspective, the higher dimensions are folded into each other, so we can't see them. But we can see them with the mind. Both physicists and spiritual sages describe the characteristics of these dimensions. Beings of every successive dimension are freed from the limitations of the one prior, but still subject to whatever limitations exist in their current dimension.

As mentioned previously, there certainly are those who can perceive dimensions beyond the usual 3, and they've been doing so for thousands of years. I feel music itself comes from another dimension, possibly more than one.

Musicians and composers: it's up to us to boldly go where none of the cats have gone before. Whether splitting atoms, infinitives or tetrachords, we have to dissect and we also have to unify. When we remember our Cause, the Effect of our music will be greatly magnified.

Reader comments

George Neidorf: Cause and effect. Jan. 12, 1958, Perth, Australia, we had just finished the set and as I was walking off the stand, I looked to my right and saw a group of Asian girls sitting at a table. One of them caught my eye and I went over to talk to her. We spent the rest of the year together until her visa expired and she returned to Thailand and I to the US. Over the next 55 yrs. I tried to find her again. One day, in 2012, I received a friend request from a young woman in Thailand. I wondered why someone I didn't know, in Thailand, wanted to friend me. I emailed back and said, if you will try to find someone for me in Bangkok, I'll "friend" you. I described the person I was looking for, her family name and social standing. She immediately emailed back and said, "Oh, you know my mother, Angelie." We married in July of 2014. Her daughter is the pianist with the Royal Bangkok Symphony.

Marco Romano: In very general terms, women perceive cyclical time more intuitively than men. They are closer to the cycles of nature like the moon's cycle.

Alki Steriopoulos: Piano key strikes wippen, jack, and hammer. A string is set in motion. Amplification by soundboard and harp carry sound vibration, through air, reaching ear, where similar mechanical process sends signal through neuron triggering response in brain. Cause and effect? I'd say.

Cause & Effect

Schrodinger's Cat, boundless possibilities existing simultaneously until one note or another is chosen, unpacked, and played. Inevitability or chance? Newtonian or Quantum Mechanics, the very nature of pre-ordained fate vs Free Will. Karma - as ye sow, so shall ye reap, (or does it?). Cervantes defines madness as seeing things as they are rather than as they might be. In Effect, Effect is causing Cause. Just Because.

Music and the 7 Hermetic Principles

HERMETIC PRINCIPLE 7:
GENDER

"Paracelsus contended that matter was a living counterpart of the creating deity. He was a dualist in that respect, for he did not share the official dogmatic opinion that God created matter the way it is described in Genesis. He believed that matter was uncreated.

These philosophers thought that in the beginning, when the spirit of God hovered over the abysmal prima materia, *she was there too and was not created. There were two things in the beginning: the male father spirit and the female matrix being, the chaotic matter...a not created but equivalent principle from the very beginning."*

–Marie-Louise von Franz, *Alchemical Active Imagination*

The 7th principle is that of Gender. The current socio/political Zeitgeist entertains the idea that there are more genders than Male and Female. Nevertheless, we must go back to the source: any variation of gender can only exist because of its roots in the Masculine and the Feminine. Without this principle, there is no Creation. Without Creation, there is no life. The very word 'gender' has a Latin root meaning "to beget; to procreate; to generate; to create; to produce."

The Kybalion goes even further into the principle with the idea of "Mental Gender," which describes not only how ideas may be put forth into the world, but also how they are received and implemented: *"The manifestation of Mental Gender may be noticed all around us in everyday life. The magnetic persons are those who are able to use the Masculine Principle in the way of impressing their ideas upon others. The actor who makes people weep. . . as he wills, is employing this principle. And so is the successful orator, statesman, preacher, writer or other people who are before the public attention. The peculiar influence exerted by some people over others is due to the manifestation of Mental Gender, along the Vibratorial lines above indicated. In this principle lies the secret of personal magnetism, personal influence, fascination, etc., as well as the phenomena generally grouped under the name of Hypnotism."*

As with all the Hermetic principles, Gender is far more than a physical reference. It may be best understood in terms of its correspondences, such as light/dark, sun/moon, strong/weak, logical/emotional and so forth.

Interactions of male and female produce a third force. This third force is what gives a vector of possibility, for without that we're stuck in the loop of duality. The feminine principle is what does the active creative work, but it must be activated by the male principle. In turn, the male principle is motivated to act because of its attraction to the female principle.

A couple of years ago I watched a video featuring a couple who built a charming cottage in the woods. The husband gave the interviewer a tour of the house and its features. Every time the interviewer commented on one of the many extraordinary details, the husband would say "Oh, Rebecca designed that....that was Rebecca's idea.....Rebecca made that in only one day...." etc. He was so proud of his wife's abilities. This is honoring the Divine Feminine– the archetypes in action! In general, the current world is lacking in this department.

Archetypes are energy patterns that exist in the collective unconscious of humanity. We see them everywhere in advertisements, the stories we read and the films we watch. Psychologists say archetypes are the secret forces behind human behavior. Plato also referred to archetypes, calling them 'forms.' Like a template, or a blueprint, they are symbolic patterns that play out over and over in media, popular culture, and human activity.

Within each male and female quality we can find more male and female subdivisions, or aspects. For starters, just below the surface of a man is his *anima*; just below the surface of a female is her *animus*. The anima is the feminine part of a man's soul; the animus is the masculine part of a woman's soul. When Carl Jung spoke about masculine and feminine archetypes, he was referring to the anima and the animus, the inner aspects, not the exterior presentation of a person. The modern interpretation is that all people have both anima and animus, in varying degrees.

We're often not aware of this hidden dimension of our psyche, but it exerts its will upon us regardless. In order to be complete souls, we have to recognize the hidden opposites within us and integrate them. Otherwise we project the archetype outside of ourselves, causing repression, and manifestation of its negative traits.

The masculine/feminine duality manifests on all levels of the human being—mentally, emotionally and physically. Therefore integration and blending of these opposites is essential. Occasionally, though, the idea of blending male/female principles has taken on a bizarre twist. In the 16th century, for example, the Vatican had banned women from singing in church choirs, creating a musical need to replace the female high voices. With its exalted tradition of vocal excellence, Italy found a unique way to deal with this situation: prepubescent boys underwent castration in order to retain their high singing voices. They became known as the *castrati*.

This practice did achieve its goal of replacing women's voices, but it came at a high price for the *castrati*, who suffered a variety of ailments due to the suppression of male hormones at such a young age. The practice was actually illegal even though quietly endorsed by the Vatican, and parents who brought their boy to the back rooms of barbers or surgeons for the procedure had to later lie and say their son was trampled by a horse, or gored by an ibex while foraging for wild mushrooms in the Dolomites.

Although a few *castrati* did achieve fame and fortune from their singing, the majority did not. The practice began to die out in the 18th century as women were once again allowed to sing in the choir. So much for the wannabe *castrati* stars of 1750…timing is everything!

Yet the attraction of the male singing voice in the female range did not die. Today falsetto singing is one of the hallmarks of male vocal pop music. In classical music men who sing in this range are known as 'countertenors.' The falsetto or countertenor range is equivalent to the female's mezzo soprano, contralto or alto.

Chinese philosophy expresses the principle of Gender with the ubiquitous *taiji* symbol, commonly known as the 'yin-yang' symbol. In this symbol the lighter color represents the Masculine while dark represents the Feminine. Yet the symbol is not static. At the most minimal point of the Masculine, an overlap into the Feminine can be seen and vice versa. At the same time, the Feminine at its fullest, most developed point, contains a dot of Masculine and vice versa. Thus the yin-yang symbol expresses not only the source of gender, Masculine and Feminine, but also expresses its combinations and transmutations.

The lack of gender equality in societies goes back thousands of years. Terence McKenna believed its root cause was in the disappearance of hallucinogenic mushrooms that grew naturally and abundantly during the Upper Paleolithic period, roughly 7,000 to 10,000 years ago. Riane Eisler, in her book *The Chalice and the Blade*—as well as McKenna in

Food of the Gods–document and explain how the rise of male 'dominator' societies then took over from the partnership societies which had been the norm wherever the magic mushrooms could be found.

Regardless of the origin of patriarchy, its existence in the world–and in the world of music–can't be denied. Whether all social problems can be attributed to this cause may be up for debate; however, all can see the world today clearly lacks balance! Sages throughout history have expounded on the need for balance in the individual, which of course extends to balance in the community, in the society, and so forth. Understanding the Hermetic Principle of Gender is a vital element in seeking and attaining this balance.

As music is always a microcosm of the outer world, we see in that realm a duplication of outward conditions. For example, equality of men and women. The modern practice of blind auditions for ensembles is not a cure-all, but it has helped rectify gender inequality somewhat. Until blind auditions became the norm, the personnel of the major symphony orchestras was entirely male despite the plethora of qualified women players. The Guardian notes, *"Even when the screen is only used for the preliminary round, it has a powerful impact; researchers have determined that this step alone makes it 50% more likely that a woman will advance to the finals. And the screen has also been demonstrated to be the source of a surge in the number of women being offered positions."*

Today's classical music world is much more egalitarian than in the past (at least in terms of gender) but that doesn't seem to extend to the jazz world. With few exceptions, headliners at jazz festivals, jazz clubs and concert venues are invariably men. Women headliners are usually singers. This is curious, as there's certainly no shortage of women instrumentalists who are making wonderful music that compares favorably with that of male musicians. (Periodic rants emerge on social media about the lack of gender equality in jazz. Invariably these posts receive a great many comments, and often reemerge months later as they're discovered by new people.)

"By the way, even a screen doesn't always yield a gender-blind event. Screens keep juries from seeing the candidates move into position, but the telltale sounds of a woman's shoes allegedly influenced some jury members such that aspiring musicians were instructed to remove their footwear before coming onto the stage."

–The Guardian

Several years ago I presented a talk at the Barron Arts Center in New Jersey, called "Do Women Play Jazz Differently Than Men?" I played a number of recorded examples of both women and men instrumentalists and invited the audience to identify their gender just by listening. Of course this was not possible (and I must admit I gave some tricky examples) unless the listener could already identify the player by ear.

My late colleague Ken Adams once remarked that the saxophone is the "last bastion of male dominance." Indeed, when I was 12 years old a male classmate told me "girls don't play the saxophone." I remember thinking *well... I play the saxophone, and I'm a girl, so obviously that's not true.* (This episode is commemorated on the track Red-haired Kid from the album Pink Slimy Worm.)

What about the trumpet, is that a 'male' instrument? We might have trouble convincing Ingrid Jensen of that, or Jaime Branch, were she still living. Trumpeter Laurie Frink was one of the first call lead players when I came up in New York. Liesl Whitaker played lead trumpet with both Army Blues and the Army Jazz Ambassadors as well as on Broadway; she now leads leads the stellar all-female trumpet section in DIVA.

And the drums, so obviously 'male'–or are they? Today's jazz drumming pantheon would be greatly diminished by the absence of Terri Lyne Carrington, Cindy Blackman, Annette Aguilar, Allison Miller, Claire Arenius, Sylvia Cuenca, Sherrie Maricle....as well as the rest of the female drummers out there, of which there are many.

Continuing along those lines, is the flute a female instrument? Disregarding the fact that all orchestral flute chairs were once occupied by men, we also have a number of distinguished male flute soloists like Galway, Rampal, Wion, Tull, Laws, et. al. whose very existence disputes such an assertion.

And don't think you're done with this issue when you die. You might be so fortunate as to be greeted at the gates of heaven by Apollo himself, performing on that oh-so-feminine of instruments, the lyre!

What are the adjectives that are used when describing music? They could include: *intense, sweet, brash, beguiling, soft, loud, forceful, gentle, aggressive, passionate, strong, emotional, nuanced*. Of these, some would be ascribed to the masculine category and others to the feminine category. Yet all these words could apply to players of either gender. If this were not so, then Melba Liston would have to be a guy and Lester Young would have to be a chick.

Music encapsulates the principle of gender because all contrasting elements, all tension and release, are expressions of masculine and feminine qualities.

Gender

The Kybalion says "*The tendency of the Feminine Principle is always in the direction of receiving impressions, while the tendency of the Masculine Principle is always in the direction of giving out, or expressing.*" We can see from this statement that music is clearly a combination of the above. A player or composer or producer must receive impressions, or creative ideas. Then those ideas must be given out, or expressed. Many people create music in their head; but unless we express it outwardly, it remains in a ghostly, un-manifested state. It lies dormant. Ideas that remain in their passive state go nowhere. Likewise, ideas only generated from superficial experiences and emotions will lack the depth needed for them to have a timeless appeal. The feminine principle needs the masculine principle and the masculine principle needs the feminine principle.

(Additionally, the act of playing music is one thing, while the process of throwing one's hat in the ring, entering the marketplace, interacting with colleagues, promoters, industry people, bandmates, is another thing altogether.)

The point is not to outwardly try to

change ourselves into our opposite, but rather to balance these opposing forces within ourselves, and become whole. It's a type of spiritual alchemy, and it's exactly the sort of thing we use our music to express. As musicians, we strive to recognize the Principle of Gender not only in ourselves, but also in our music. Without expressing both masculine and feminine elements our music will never be able to communicate a timeless, universal quality.

    The music world is still male-dominated, as many fields are. Which is odd, because music itself has no gender. But it does use the *principle* of gender. The Principle of Gender is absolutely indispensable to the construction and performance of music. Let us well acquaint ourselves with it, and be better musicians as well as better human beings as a result.

Reader comments

Dillon Vado: I agree with you that there is tremendous imbalance in our culture and that does start with our individuals. I think men in particular do need to hear and read this kind of message.

Marco Romano: it is readily apparent that women are the future. You can see it in the abortion issue, in the horrible acts done to women around the world and in other forms of oppression.

Alki Steriopoulos: As a straight male working as a Musical Director in NYC I can assure you, socio-gender discrimination was not a one-way street. I was told more than once that not being in "the boys club," made career advancement unlikely, if not impossible. Likewise, the women that were successful in the field tended to be tougher than their male counterparts, perhaps imagining they had to be. The gender dance has been with us since Goddess took a rib from Adam and improved upon the model. Hopefully the Pendulum of Extremes will snap back to center one day where talent alone is the only yardstick. And who knows? Maybe then a new archetype called a Human Being will be created. One in which gender will be a distant secondary consideration.

Music and the 7 Hermetic Principles

AFTERWORD

The concepts presented in this book may be new to you. Delving into them, you'll get closer to whatever mysterious source gives us music in the first place. These ideas are not intellectual exercises, but rather an invitation to explore music's hidden pathways, as well as the path of our own inner being.

Medical students dissect animal and human corpses. A fledgeling clockmaker takes clocks apart and puts them back together. Similarly, musicians examine each of the elements and concepts of music in order to better understand how music works, not only in the physical world but in the metaphysical realm as well.

The understanding we gain in this process gives us a deeper knowledge of music, helps us play better, and allows us to transmit our music to listeners more effectively. We can also apply it to our compositional process.

Perhaps most importantly, our deep investigation into music's source and meaning is what makes our music truly human. It is a path with heart, and no machine will ever be able to follow it.

Let's always remember that the gift of being musical is one many people wish they had, not realizing the depth of the journey and the responsibilities it contains. When we discover more about music, we discover more about ourselves. By navigating life as musicians, we are able to go places that are closed off to others—literally, figuratively, and spiritually.

Music is the perfect microcosm of life, and we're privileged to play our way through it. All of us, together, make a band that is more than the sum of its parts.

Let's lead the parade into humanity's new era.

ACKNOWLEDGEMENTS

I want to thank those readers who took the time to comment on this book as the chapters appeared in serial form at Temple of Artists.

Every writer of philosophy wishes for an educated and insightful readership. I am honored that the following people have contributed their thoughts and impressions to this book:

Marco Romano
George Neidorf
Connie Cheng
Mary-Lou
Nina Ott
Mark Ax
Alki Steriopoulos
Susan Hart
Bud Revels
Dillon Vado

When it came time to consider an author for the Foreword I thought deeply about which of my colleagues would be able to comment on the topic effectively, and passionately.

There was one person who stood out in this regard. He is not only a formidable musician and composer, but also a profound writer. He's one of today's most vital shakuhachi masters and I consider him a mentor as well as a friend. He was my first choice for author of the foreword, and as the heavens would have it, he said yes!

Thank you, dear Cornelius Boots, for adding your uniqueness to this effort.

I'm grateful for my wonderful and brilliant husband, writer Johnny Jara Jaramillo. Where would I be but for his sage advice and support of my projects. . . plus, he keeps me laughing. *Gracias, mi amor, por todo!*

ABOUT THE AUTHOR

Photo by James Richard Kao

Su Terry is a composer, soloist and recording artist on saxophone, clarinet and shakuhachi.

She has performed and recorded with a long list of music VIPs and has been a jazz soloist with several national and international symphony orchestras.

She specializes in the integration of music, metaphysics and spirituality.

More information can be found in the books *Reed All About It* by Bob Bernotas, *Madame Jazz* by Leslie Gourse; *Experiencing Jazz* by Michael Stephans, *Penguin Guide to Jazz on CD*, and *All Music Guide*.

Su Terry is a Yamaha Saxophone Artist. She plays Jody Jazz mouthpieces and ligatures, and Légère reeds.

Website
suterry.com

Recordings
qinote.bandcamp.com

Weekly articles and podcasts
templeofartists.substack.com

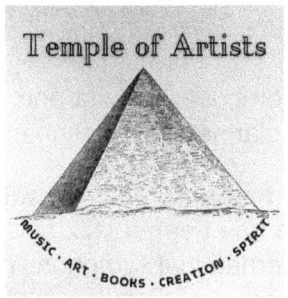

By the same author

Inside the Mind of a Musician

For The Curious

I Was a Jazz Musician For the FBI

Instruction books

Practice Like The Pros

Step One: Play Alto Sax

Step One: Play Tenor Sax

Step One: Play Clarinet

www.ingramcontent.com/pod-product-compliance
Lightning Source LLC
Chambersburg PA
CBHW060157050426
42446CB00013B/2868